RING$
OF
VALUE

RUN YOUR BUSINESS EVERY DAY
LIKE IT'S FOR SALE

TIMOTHY M. BEGLIN, CPA

Testimonials For Ring$ of Value

If you are really serious about growing your business value or if you ever think you may want to sell your company, grab the Ring$ of Value, devour it, and reap the reward!
—Stephen B. Monyer, Managing Partner, AmCheck Merchant Services

Tim Beglin has connected on something here that is really powerful. Our company is living proof. With the Ring$ of Value as our target, we focus on the things that actually drive growth and millions of dollars in business value. My advice . . . read this book and put Tim's concepts into action before your competition does.
—Lynne Wallace, Co-Founder and CEO, VANTREO

In his book Ring$ of Value, Tim Beglin gives business owners and entrepreneurs the opportunity to unshackle themselves from the day-to day workings of their businesses to focus on building real long-term value that can be realized in the marketplace. Tim delivers his message in a voice that is familiar and easily accessible.
—Larry Goldberg, Partner, ESOP Law Group, LLP

I have found that the principles in Ring$ of Value give us the necessary business levers needed to be competitive in today's international marketplace.
—Chris Hsu, President, China Operations, HB Sourcing International

Ring$ of Value is an incredible resource. Think of it as your guidebook to unleashing the true value of your company, regardless of your industry—how much is that worth to you?
—Bob Reynolds, CPA, Co-Founder and CFO of Innovative Business Solutions, Inc.

Tim Beglin writes about complex business valuation concepts in a clear and concise way. As a practitioner, there is no fluff here, just usable information to help you drive value in your company.
—Josh Edwards, ASA, Managing Director, Eureka Valuation Advisors

This book was a real eye-opener. These simple yet powerful concepts will turn even a medical doctor into a savvy businessperson.
—James C. Devore, MD, Family Physician, Medical Director of the Annadel Medical Group, Expert Consultant for the Medical Board of California, and Author of White Coat Wrinkle

Ring$ of Value is a must-read for anyone thinking about or aspiring to own a business. I know, because that was me. These principles have given our company the necessary tools and direction to build a strong foundation and to be competitive in the retail industry.
—Noah Lowry, Entrepreneur and Former MLB Pitcher

I am not aware of another book on the market that actually guides the reader on how to drive the value of a business. This is a must-read for any business owner or entrepreneur who wants clear direction on how to elevate into a higher Ring of strategic thinking. These concepts have really worked in my companies!
—Steve Farmiloe, Founder, Alpha Enterprises

To have joy, excitement, and hope for your business is imperative. If your business has lost its way, I strongly recommend you read this book, for it will help you revive your dream!
—Kimberly Zink, President and CEO, Klemmer & Associates Premier Leadership Organization, and Author of I Love Me, I Love Me Not

If you own a business or want to take it to the next level, then do yourself and your company a favor and read Ring$ of Value. It is the most important book about adding value to your business to come along in years.
—Manny Goulart, President, Goulart Partners

After reading Ring$ of Value, my best advice to my clients will be for them to read this book!

—Rick Roehm, MBA Owner and President, Money Masters Financial Group

If you want to make your company more valuable, this book is a must-read! In fact, read it a few times to make sure you got everything out of your own valuation.

—Pete Gilfillan, FranChoice Consultant and Best-Selling Author of Hire Yourself

Ring$ of Value is truly an informative book. It walks the reader through easily understandable and actionable steps that should help enhance the value of any business.

—John Wepler, Chairman and CEO, Marsh, Berry & Company, Inc.

This book is so timely. I have been in business for some time and involved in several deals, but have never been able to find this kind of resource. This book really nails it. Wish I had it earlier in my career!

—Nate Shelton, Chief Marketing Officer, Driven Performance Brands, including Hurst and Flowmaster products; Specialty Equipment Market Association (SEMA) Hall of Fame

Ring$ of Value is a must-read for any business owner who wants to get a grasp of the value of his or her business. Not only does it provide an easy to understand formula to derive value, it also explains the key drivers of that value. Tim has taken a career of learning and wrapped it all up between the covers of an exceptionally easy to read book. It doesn't matter if someone is trying to buy a business, sell a business, or simply value a business, Ring$ of Value takes the complex, not easy to understand valuation process and makes it understandable. The book should be in the top drawer of every business owner's desk!

—James S. Jackson, CEO, Harman Management Corporation (the first and largest franchisee of Kentucky Fried Chicken)

Timothy M. Beglin / Ring$ of Value
Printed in the United States of America

Ring$ of Value / Timothy M. Beglin -- 1st ed.

ISBN 978-0-9971556-0-0 Print Edition
ISBN 978-0-9971556-1-7 Ebook Edition

CONTENTS

Explore Your Passion, Find Your Ring, Embrace The Journey.

FOREWORD

Do you run a business? Do you want to make more money? Do you operate in a competitive environment? Do you want customers to continue to see value and remain with your business? Do you want employees who are committed to and proud of where they work? Do you want this business to provide for your retirement and possibly help your children? If you answer yes to even one of these questions, then read this book, *Rings of Value*. It will help you achieve your goals!

I have known the author of this book, Tim Beglin, for a long time. From the first time I met Tim, I saw a guy who was inquisitive. This attribute continued to develop over time, and for many years now it has defined Tim. One of the reasons he became a certified public accountant (CPA) is that it allowed him a front row seat to business. He was able to see businesses from a very intimate vantage point, and he could figure out each puzzle by asking, What is the business model? Who are the competitors? How does this business make money, generate cash, and earn a profit? Tim is always trying to figure out the puzzle—it's part of his natural curiosity, but a larger part is his desire to understand how to make a business better.

There are millions of businesses in this country, and usually the business owners are very focused on the day-to-day issues staring them in the face. Many are very focused on the challenge of generating sales each day, but they are not trained in strategic thinking or the process of strategic evaluation. But to have a truly

successful business, you must spend a little more time being strategic and a little less time with tactical execution. *Rings of Value*
helps you think about your business in a different way, one that
can allow you to run your business better and create more value,
satisfaction, and pride.

There are many reasons to operate a business—to follow your
dream, to be your own boss, to create income and a better living,
to provide good jobs to your employees, etc. Another reason is to
create wealth for yourself and others. This wealth creation will
allow you to retire, help your children through college, pass some
wealth onto your family members, or perhaps be philanthropic.
Rings of Value helps business owners think about their business
differently. It offers easy steps and practical suggestions for how
to do this to create more value and wealth. Tim's model asks you
to manage your business more effectively so you can monetize
this asset at some point in time and have a better business in the
process.

This is a great guide for any business owner. It represents a
small investment that can reap a large reward. The tools in this
book can help you lead or manage your business better. The reward could be an improved sales- or service-delivery process, a
higher functioning management team, monetary gain . . . or all of
the above.

Like Tim, I also started my career as a CPA and enjoyed seeing
a number of businesses up close, through my invitations to advise
the management teams. After leaving public accounting, I went on
to work for and eventually lead a variety of businesses. The first
one was a public company, and later divisions of a large New York
Stock Exchange business. In the publicly traded company world,
the concept of leading and managing the business for the long
term while creating short-term shareholder value was drilled into
me every month and quarter. There is a lot of tension in "growing

profitably"—growing the top and bottom lines to increase share-holder value, along with all the short-term trade-offs you have to manage to achieve this objective. Many private businesses have the luxury of the long game, but they also miss the pressure and discipline of really focusing on shareholder value. *Rings of Value* provides many practical tools to help a business owner do both, but requires a commitment to stick to the process and change your way of thinking, leading, and managing.

Commit to being more strategic following the steps outlined in *Rings of Value* along with the discipline to follow them for the long term. The end result can be very fulfilling and rewarding.

Scott J. Cromie

Chairman of the Board and CEO

2-10 Home Buyers Warranty

(formerly Group President of The ServiceMaster Company)

INTRODUCTION

Picture yourself as an aspirant on the highly popular TV show *Shark Tank*. You're one of the enterprising individuals standing before the panel of potential investors (known for entertainment purposes as "the Sharks") and presenting your entrepreneurial vision in the hope of convincing one or more of them to put real money into your business.

Typically presenters start out by telling the panel about themselves, their business concept, and their hopes and aspirations for the business's success. A product demonstration then follows. Generally this portion of the presentation goes pretty well. As with most entrepreneurs, the presenters are by and large comfortable, relating their story and talking up their business idea.

Next comes the dramatic tension of the show, when the Sharks begin to ask questions pertinent to the financial or operational aspects of the presenter's business. This is where you see who really understands the economics of their business and, in particular, who really knows how to value a business. Business investment is not about hollow projections or wishful thinking but is rather the creation of value that goes beyond just the bottom line.

This book is intended to prepare you for a similar conversation when you get into your own *Shark Tank*–type negotiations. Whether you are in manufacturing, wholesale or retail, service or technology, there is significant financial benefit in knowing how potential investors think. As a business owner, you need to know what kind of information they are looking for and how they truly perceive value. Most likely it's not what you think. To be blunt, investors are not interested in your sacrifices, your sweat equity, or how long you have been pursuing your dream. Moreover, they have very little interest in knowing what *you* think your business is worth. A potential buyer, investor, or partner is only interested in the calculation of the actual monetary value of the enterprise— it's just dollars and cents.

My objective in writing this book was to pass along how businesses are actually valued in a sales transaction. The vision was to format the book in an interesting yet challenging way for owners and entrepreneurs so they would realize that their role as CEO is to grow and sustain their businesses by continually adding value. Financially speaking, conversations with potential investors come down to value. With this book, I am letting you in on some of the well-kept secrets of business valuation. By knowing these secrets and using them to *your* advantage, you can actually drive up the value of your company far beyond its current market ceiling. Further, with this knowledge you can build a sustainable organization that allows you freedoms you may not have previously realized.

The real valuation of one's business and, just as important, what drives that valuation is a proven formula that most business owners are either not aware of or, if they are, do not truly understand how it can be used to their advantage. Why? Because their focus is working *in* their business rather than *on* their business—the exact opposite of what actually drives enterprise value!

Now you may be thinking that you have no immediate plans to sell your business or to attract outside investment; that's okay.

An important takeaway here is that if you run your business every day like it's for sale, then this allows you to identify opportunities, pursue innovations, and explore channels of thought and information that your competitors aren't even considering. It allows you to create a platform of growth and change that will spearhead your place at the head of your industry. Here's the catch: To run your business every day like it's for sale requires a new and broader vision in your thinking. Are you ready for the challenge?

————

By viewing your day-to-day operations with even the idea of a potential sale in mind, your focus shifts from the likes of tracking daily sales and whether or not a particular invoice got paid to a higher strategic level that can have an exponential impact on the overall value of your company.

————

Think home ownership for a moment. Consider how a house seemingly never looks as good as when the owners put it up for sale. If they want top dollar, everything must look impeccable. They freshen up the lawn and gardens, fix any plumbing leaks, put on a fresh coat of paint, and update the kitchen to make it eye catching.

Now imagine a similar mindset regarding the business you currently own or the one you're considering starting. When buyers come looking, they want to see signs of diligent care. They want to see a smooth-running operation and a solid financial foundation. They also want to see that a strong culture has been established and that the owners have an eye on innovation, growth, and a commitment to their community.

A house in pristine condition gives a prospective buyer added confidence that you, as the owner, have pride of ownership in caring for your property. It lends energy and momentum to any potential transaction. It adds worth beyond the other homes in the neighborhood. It suggests that you have treated your home with care every day. It is not an accident that this house sells more quickly and for a surprisingly higher amount than others in the neighborhood.

Maximizing the appeal of your business in the eyes of an investor or buyer is similar to caring for your house as the investment that it is. Whether it is your business or your home, you want to make the very best impression you can. Taking the best possible care of your house is not a last-minute task; instead it needs to be a conscious choice, part of your home-owner hygiene. Running your business every day as if you're going to sell it is exactly the same. Your operational processes must be documented and sound, your business assets need to be productive, and your comprehension of your company finances and industry dynamics must be so thorough that you communicate them fluidly.

All true. But there is even more to it than that. Much more.

As a business owner, you have to move beyond the day-to-day intricacies that consume you from the moment you get up in the morning to a place where *value* is defined as a currency that elevates every decision you make. As the title of this book suggests, I call this place the Rings of Value.

Understanding the dynamics inside each of these Rings of Value will serve to clarify which of the multitude of your "to-do's" are really valuable to your business and thus worth expending your limited time on each day.

The bottom line is that an understanding of the elements within the Rings of Value will make your business far more desirable to a potential buyer or investor than the competitor who is selling a similar product or marketing a like service.

Throughout my early career as a CPA, and later in my numerous C-level positions and during my time as a business consultant,

I helped guide companies both large and small. I have been involved in many successful mergers and acquisitions (including some involving internationally recognizable names). From these vast experiences in advising, restructuring, and strategizing, I have developed a straightforward, comprehensive, and effective process to enhance the value of any business—**including yours**.

Whether you are a business owner, company stakeholder, or would-be entrepreneur, the purpose of this book is to give you an insider's knowledge of just how businesses are valued so that you can maximize the rewards of your invested time and sweat equity.

Consider this your roadmap for building lasting value.

———

Tony Robbins, self-help guru/executive coach, often says, "Complexity is the enemy of execution." He also says, "The key to converting what I learn into something useful to others is simplicity."

———

I couldn't agree more. The processes I share in this book are deceptively simple. Simple, however, does not mean easy. Moreover, the success of these processes requires you to be brutally honest with yourself about how you run your company and how you define value. For my part, I promise not to bore you with tedious talk of debits and credits or overcumbersome narratives about balance sheets and income statements. I will, however, need you to absorb the few yet extremely vital formulas and theories that I do present.

As you work your way through these specifically designed exercises targeted solely to prepare you to fully understand the potential impact of Ring$ of Value on your business, imagine your dream investor is sitting across the table from you asking the same probing questions the Sharks would. Will you be prepared? More than that, will your responses be so conversant and knowledgeable as to garner their time, interest, and, most important, money?

I believe the preparation tools you will need to succeed in just such a *Shark Tank*–type moment are contained within these pages.

Let's begin your transformation!

CHAPTER 1

WHERE REAL VALUE BEGINS

As an owner in a business, you probably spend a great deal of your time every day solving problems and running the nuts and bolts of your company. On one hand, these are very likely necessary activities meant to move your business forward; on the other hand, resolving routine customer issues, spending an excessive amount of time in meetings, or fixing faulty pipes won't necessarily propel you ahead of your competitors. It is fairly certain that these daily activities won't make your business as profitable as it can be, and isn't profit one of the primary reasons we all started our companies? As the ten and twelve hour days tick by, I recommend you ask yourself this question: **What are you doing above and beyond the norm to increase the overall value of your enterprise?** What steps are you taking to make sure that your business is the very best it can possibly be, both in your eyes and the eyes of the outside world?

The only way to effectively track this progress is to measure actual value. However, the truth is, many business owners do not possess the necessary tools to arrive at a valuation number. They reach a point where they want to sell what they've built or seek outside investment to take what they've built to the next level, and they have no idea how much their hard work is actually worth.

That's why I wrote this book. Contained within these pages are fast calculation tools meant to measure real value, seven of the most potent means of increasing real value, and plenty of words of guidance, caution, and encouragement. I want you, the reader and the most important person in this discussion, to see that you have more power than you've been led to believe in influencing the ultimate valuation of your business. You do not have to be, nor should you be a victim of so-called industry standards. You can learn the same tricks the insiders use to positively affect real value and take a seat at a *Shark Tank*–type table with confidence. (See the Introduction to learn more about how the *Shark Tank* TV show relates to business valuation.)

I've been on both sides of the acquisition table. I have helped business owners in a variety of industries through the process. I know which qualities end up netting a profit and which do not. I know what high-level investors are looking for. I know the strategies they employ to take the current operating levels of a business and make them infinitely more profitable and valuable.

I want to help you learn these techniques too, not because I'm suggesting you sell what you've built—though that exit strategy may be one you consider at some point—but because operating your business as if someone *were* going to buy it imposes discipline. It challenges your creativity and your innovation. Making decisions about everyday problems with elevated value in mind changes the game. Knowing where to spend your time and money becomes a bit easier when you can clearly see what activities will eventually net the most profit and add real value and what activities are just keeping you busy. That's why this book is subtitled *Run Your Business Every Day Like It's For Sale*. It is a mindset that will help you envision a more profitable future. It is very important to note here that such a mindset does not constitute a quick fix; in fact, changing attitudes requires time and practice. In the end, however, when you run your business every day like it's for sale you see your company's potential in an entirely new way.

Paired with your new mindset comes a series of actionable tools. I call them the Ring$ of Value. Learned through many years of experience, the Rings represent characteristics, strategies, and tactics that the most successful businesses on my resume possessed and implemented. They are the qualities that attract outside interest and eventual investment because they increase the value of your business in ways that are not inherent in the everyday operations of most of your competitors.

Codified into a series of Rings, this valuable insider information includes strategies that the most successful businesspeople employ, even if the terms they use are slightly different from the ones noted in the Ring$ of Value. By learning and utilizing these key valuation tools, you can make the same enhancements to your own company as they have to theirs. So instead of an investor reaping those enhanced profits, you get to keep them yourself.

Free Yourself from the Noise

Pictured here are two disparate ways of doing business.

The first one is standard operating procedure for most of us; that is, we focus on the day-to-day operations. We focus on sales and marketing, customer and employee relations, vendors, expense management, and ongoing to-do lists.

The second way of doing business includes strategies you can and should be developing **beyond the day-to-day operations**. Each layer of this strategy, individually or collectively, is essential to enhancing your business value and outwitting the valuation multiplier predetermined by industry standards for all the businesses in your market niche.

As shown below in Figure 1, your daily to-do list equals what I call "business noise": meetings, HR issues, competitor concerns, etc. While all are a necessary part of business, they will take you away from the endeavors that will really and truly increase the value of your business.

Of course these responsibilities are all critical to the success of your business. No one is suggesting otherwise. You can't skip them. But you do have options. You can, for example, delegate some of them. You can relegate some of them to certain hours of the day or certain days of the week.

The bottom line is this: If you're going to add the kind of value that investors or potential buyers are highly attuned to, you're going to have to move beyond the noise and into the Ring$ of Value.

Figure 1: Your Distractions

Business Noise
- Day-to-day tasks
- Meetings, returning phone calls or emails
- Business concerns/risks
- Sales forecasts
- Budgets and cash flows
- Increasing overhead expenses
- Lawsuits

- Bank financing
- Vendor pricing/delivery problems
- Management team strengths and weaknesses
- Staffing and HR issues
- The speed of changes in technology
- To-do lists
- Deadlines
- Competition!

Figure 2: Your Goal

This is the target I want you to hold in your mind:

Knowing about the target is one thing, but getting onto it is a real win. So, welcome and congratulations—it's more than your competitors are probably accomplishing. From here, each Ring of the target represents an element beyond the day-to-day business noise that will impact the real value of your business.

As an overview, the way the following Rings enhance your business's value is in reverse order of their presentation. The outermost Ring has a very positive impact on overall value but a lesser amount relative to the next one in line, and so on and so on, all the way inward to the center Ring, which can have **the most incremental impact on your enterprise value**. It's possible (and very common) to see businesses utilizing multiple Rings simultaneously.

I will go into each in a lot more detail later, but for now here is a very brief overview of these incredibly powerful Ring$ of Value, beginning with the outermost Ring:

7. Cultural Environment

The objective here is to create a company culture so magnetic that workers are drawn to it, that it positively influences the loyalty of existing employees, the energy of the management team, and the interest level of shareholders. Companies with such a desirable cultural environment continually attract value-adding performers.

This self-perpetuating organism, realized by creating and reinforcing an environment within your company that compellingly attracts the most talented level of employee, the strongest and deepest management team, combined with the most distinctive and active level of shareholders, is the closest thing to perpetual motion in business. Companies with just such a desirable culture attract high performers, who continue to attract other like performers, and the cycle continues. Examples of these types of cultural environment companies would be Disney and Google.

6. Innovation

The company identities in this Ring are based on innovation and, most important, stepping beyond the status quo because of this ingenuity (perhaps to the point of a positive industry disruption). Their product or service continuum is far beyond that of the competition and makes them the standard-bearer of their industry, no matter what the organizational size.

The creativity and marketplace success of these innovations have really become what these companies are known for—it is who they are. Their products or services are not only revolutionary, they perhaps have a bit of an edge to them as well. These companies are clearly industry innovation leaders that are setting the pace and direction for any others that deem themselves to be in the same niche. Companies such as Apple come to mind as just such idea-based innovators.

5. Revenue Streams

Business revenue can be dissected like a freeway intersection coming in from many different directions. How can revenue be defined in any way other than what it is, you ask? Well, it is all in the eye of the beholder, which is what makes this Ring and these diverse companies more valuable than their fellow competitors.

A *revenue stream* refers to methods by which money comes in to a company. There doesn't appear to be any limit to that definition, does there? That is why I want you to think of revenue in its broadest terms, coming in various forms, including diversification into completely new product lines or brand-new add-on service revenue sources.

Take Tesla, for example. Apparently it is not enough that the company turned the entire auto industry on its head with its innovation, but now in their Gigafactory they will be mass-producing the lithium ion battery with their manufacturing partners. This advancement is not only going to lower Tesla's own production costs, it could also avail these lower-cost batteries to the mass market—providing Tesla with a whole new revenue stream!

4. Distribution Channels

A well-established logistical system takes time, experience, and is extremely costly to develop but oh so valuable to investors. Whether your company has an international sourcing and importing network or a domestic distribution center/warehousing operation with an integrated trucking or railway labyrinth, the ability to economically and efficiently move product from point A to point B is money to an investor. Grainger comes to mind, a logistical octopus. Anything in the tool and supply/safety industry can be found in their legendary Grainger catalog. Of course, *the* best example of today's leader in the distribution channel industry is Amazon, a company that has products at your front door almost before you hit "Add to Cart" on their website. The companies that have focused on and perfected the distribution chain model can realize enormous valuation multipliers from investors.

3. Branding and Public Identification

Why will consumers pay more for a certain product brand versus another? Aren't all running shoes really about the same? Aren't most of them made overseas by the same or similar factories? Then why do so many consumers identify with the Nike brand/logo over another shoe? The reason is that beyond the performance of the item, there are intangible social and psychological reasons consumers buy one brand over another.

Or how about when that small teal box is presented? *Everyone* in the room recognizes it as a Tiffany box. That simple yet elegant packaging has so much emotional adrenaline and anticipation packed into it, at times even beyond the actual item itself. This level of international brand recognition is an investor's dream because of the inherently higher gross profit margins and worldwide sales opportunities. Operating metrics for companies in this Ring can perform far beyond any non-branded competitor.

2. Ability to Replicate and Scale

Although these expandable enterprises exist in nearly every industry, for an initial definition of this highly valued Ring, think of the fast-food convenience model. Your Starbucks grande triple-shot latte is the same in Seattle as it is Singapore. Anywhere throughout the world, the Starbucks system, recipes, and experience look, feel, and taste the same. Create a product or service that can be replicated and scaled, and you will have the special attention of investors because of the numerical power of its expansion capability and the relatively calculable return on investment (ROI). An enterprise like Starbucks will have the exact dollar amount for how much a new location costs, what its operating costs will be, along with vast daily expected sales data for the new store. Therefore, Starbucks corporate or any potential investor in this type of replicable and scalable operation can fairly accurately forecast the compounding effect of adding new locations.

1. Power to Change Lives

This is the center of the target! Why? Because it's the apex, where the entrepreneurial spirit meets the investment community. Does your company's identity have the power to change lives? Equally important, does your company's social consciousness cross over and translate to your income statement to become an enormous goodwill add-on valuation factor? For example, TOMS Shoes donates a pair of shoes for every new pair purchased. Whether intentional or not, such companies have built extraordinary value by combining really, really good products with an ability to simultaneously effect social awareness and change. The power to change lives exponentially changes the way investors view the value of your organization.

***

When investors or potential buyers witness any of these seven action avenues at work, they see a company far more valuable than its competitors. For those very talented companies that can engage in multiple Rings simultaneously, holy smokes can their valuations jump! Investors see an entity they are anxious to invest in because the owner or owners aren't running it like their "same old, same old" competitors.

Accomplished companies are engaged in a Ring or two, but don't limit yourself. **How many Rings can your company be engaged in to increase your company's value?**

What Is Your Business Really Worth?

When you run your business every day like it's for sale and engage in the Ring$ of Value, you understand that what you think your company is worth may not be the same as the value assessment a potential buyer or interested investor might make.

So when asked the question "What is your business really worth?" you have to be clear that the way you calculate value is founded in logic and supportable to any interested outsiders. Beyond that, it is even more important that you be as well versed as possible in the added measures that you can make to actually increase that value.

Enter the Ring$ of Value!

Each business owner has a vision of the value of his or her company, much like you do for your business or the business you hope to own someday. However, beware. When you approach a venture capitalist (VC) or private equity group about a sale or an infusion of capital, the potential investor rarely views this valuation in the same way you do.

These experienced business buyers or investors will very often make their initial assessment in minutes, not days, relying on years of experience, plenty of successes, and the inevitable failures. It can take years for entrepreneurs to build the kind of intrinsic value that separates their business from the competition in terms of the cultural environment they have created, their distribution channels, brand identification, or the scalability of their product or services (all elements of the Ring$ of Value) but mere moments for experienced investment experts to spot it. Once a particular investor is interested, there are few if any second chances for making that transaction, so **you have to be ready**!

Business owners who have diligently imbued their ventures with the right kind of value—value established by stepping beyond the day-to-day noise of their operations—always stand a better chance of walking away with a sale or an infusion of capital from an investment partner. If you've watched the show *Shark Tank*, then you realize that many of these hopeful entrepreneurs settle for much less than they had hoped for or anticipated, and some walk away with no deal at all. Although *Shark Tank* is a reality TV show, the financial ramifications of wooing a prospective buyer or looking for an investment partner for your business are surprisingly not that different in the real world.

———

In his book *How to Win at the Sport of Business*, Mark Cuban (one of the Sharks on the show) says, "One problem people have is that they lie to themselves . . . rarely is talent enough. You have to find ways to make yourself stand out."

———

I interpret Mr. Cuban's words this way: Owners and entrepreneurs *have* to engage in a high level of commitment to accomplish what needs to be done every day—that's understandable—but it's this pie-in-the-sky optimism that inevitably causes so many business owners and would-be entrepreneurs to overestimate their enterprise's value.

Be aware: Your investors, if and when you decide to sell your business or seek outside funding, will not be taking this same over-the-top optimistic valuation view.

When I say you should run your business every day like it's for sale, I am *not* implying that you will necessarily be selling it in the next year or even the next five years. What I am implying is that you understand what is valuable to a potential buyer. Then, when and if you do decide to seek outside investment at some point or create an exit strategy that includes the sale of your business, you can support your proposed valuation with those absolutely essential facts, metrics, and industry comparables.

When potential investors in a business venture opt out, it is normally because they see business owners or would-be entrepreneurs who lack the ability to step out of the shadows of their competitors and elevate their enterprises beyond the ordinary.

In my years in the business world, I've seen it all, and the Ring$ of Value concept has grown out of harsh realities that separate diligence and hard work from the kind of effort that is as innovative as it is diligent and as forward thinking as it is committed. I've been involved in companies that sold quickly and at a premium and others that brought the owners exactly what the going industry standards said they would get. The companies that propelled their valuations beyond the industry norm were inevitably ventures that had invested resources in the Ring$ of Value. **Which do you want to be?**

I decided to write this book to pass this insider information on to business owners and entrepreneurs like you, to help you better understand the process and the drivers of business valuation.

Ringing Truths

The Ring$ of Value list is my own secret interpretational approach for magnifying the value of your enterprise *beyond* your industry standard multiples.

My goal is to provide you with valuation secrets that will convert your ordinary business sale into an extraordinary one that exceeds your wildest financial expectations.

While we will get deeper into implementing the Ring$ of Value concepts later in the book, for now I wanted to leave you with one thought: **Instead of asking what your business is today, ask what can it be?**

Chapter 1 Takeaways

1. The knowledge required to successfully negotiate a business transaction is not just for the experienced professional. It is within your grasp—and within these pages!

2. Yes, you have to take good care of the business noise to have a successful business, but stepping above the noise and into the Rings is where the true enhanced value of your business is created.

3. Learn the Ring$ of Value, for they, paired with a solid understanding of the valuation formula, which you'll discover in the next chapter, are the levers you can pull to increase your business's value exponentially.

CHAPTER 2

THE ABCs OF BUSINESS VALUATION

When you sell your business, you want to maximize its value, don't you? If so, then you must have the *right* buyer. The concept sounds so simple, yet many sellers overlook it—to their own financial chagrin. In other words, if your business is a must-have for a potential buyer, then they will be more inclined to pay full value (or perhaps even more) for it versus someone else who may have a more casual interest in owning it. So, before we get into the actual dollars and cents about business valuations, it is essential that you **know your audience**. Who are the mysterious buyers out there that you might encounter in the selling process? Knowing your buyer's DNA is as necessary as knowing your ABCs before you can begin to read.

The good news is that the list is concise and to the point. There are only three typical buyer profiles: Emotional Buyers, Strategic Buyers, and Financial Buyers/Investors. Let's briefly introduce each in order:

Emotional Buyer – Sometimes a buyer falls in love with a business and just has to have it. Perhaps they have dreamed of owning a restaurant, clothing store, or some type of service business. It happened for me once. During my son's Little League baseball days, I started taking him to an indoor batting facility to practice his hitting. I loved the concept. The facility provided baseball and softball players a place to work on their hitting year-round, rain or shine. One day I happened to start a conversation with one of the owners. His partner was getting a divorce and was looking to sell his half of the business. I told him I might be interested, and, in a matter of a few weeks, I was the proud partner of half of an indoor batting facility. Was the facility destined to make me a bunch of money? Probably not. Was it something I was proud to be a part of and that gave me the pride of ownership? Absolutely. Would I run it with an eye on increasing its value? Most definitely!

Emotional buyers use different criteria in their business search. They typically don't have much experience in high-level investment, so they may not know to ask *Shark Tank*–like questions. When these types of deals happen, they generally happen quickly. It's also hard to quantify these emotional buyers because their transactions are not largely publicized. An Under New Management sign may appear in the window of their new establishment or an announcement may be posted on their website, but generally operations continue unabated and, hopefully, with success similar to or better than what the previous owner experienced.

The bottom line, however, is that emotional buyers are not your primary buyer audience; one might come along, but they're not likely to understand the true value of your enterprise.

At the batting cages, we did develop enough value-added services to ultimately turn a pretty good profit. We created a skill-enhancing environment for players by introducing professional hitting lessons from former professional baseball players. We featured off-season hitting leagues, and we offered birthday parties and other events that helped build a positive reputation in the area. I may have been an emotional buyer to begin with, but the enjoyment I took from this small yet very personal endeavor turned at some point into a drive to make it financially successful too. That is the beauty of the emotional buyer: They tend to give 100 percent, and that very often gives balance to their transactional inexperience.

In the end, our efforts caught the attention of some qualified investors who ended up buying the facility at a very nice price as the anchor of a franchising idea they were promoting.

Which leads me to buyer profile number two:

Strategic Buyers – Very often this type of buyer is already operating in your business sector or in one with connections to your industry. Their familiarity with the industry means that they understand the marketplace and have an existing operating structure in place to support further business volume. Because of the projected synergies, these buyers are *strategic*, meaning their plan is to incorporate your business into their operations. By combining your business with theirs, the strategic buyer expects to create a higher return on investment than a standalone business could provide. The same way my batting cage attracted the attention of those investors with their franchise idea, strategic buyers are trying to develop or expand their existing market share and may see your business as just the right addition.

Let's suppose that you own an independent veterinary clinic, have nurtured a strong and loyal clientele, and have created a profitable working model. A well-funded veterinary group that may have or want to have a larger presence in the region (or in an area nearby) might consider buying your practice to help expand the group's market share into this territory. This expansion strategy is quite common for a strategic buyer.

The key point in recognizing strategic buyers is that they are already participating in your industry. They may be located elsewhere, but they are familiar with the operational aspects of the industry and generally will already have the administrative base and background to add the incremental volume of this new acquisition to their existing operation. This "incremental volume" aspect is key, because, generally speaking, strategic buyers can afford and will usually pay a higher purchase price for a business because their projected ROI is higher due to the inherent synergies.

Lastly, buyer profile number three:

Financial Buyers/Investors – These are the Sharks: the venture capitalists, the private equity firms, and the experienced investors. These folks are generally drawn to make a purchase based on whether the numbers fit their very strict ROI and risk objectives. Equally important is whether or not there is a way for them to integrate your business into a fund of other like businesses, with the ultimate goal of either packaging said businesses together to be sold as a unit or breaking them up and reselling them separately.

A brief definition of these key financial players is helpful here. Venture capitalists (VCs), or "angel investors," as they are often called, are generally the early-stage investors in a business. They are the ones you hear about investing in start-up companies, for example. VCs generally get into a deal early—that is, before significant or steady revenues and profits are realized. Therefore, as a valuation strategy, VCs' investment model will include pricing influences for their targeted ROI and their assumption of risk. Since both their ROI requirements and inherent risk of an early-stage investment are high, VCs' valuations of companies will tend to be on the lower end of a pricing spectrum to compensate for these factors.

On the other hand, private equity groups tend to get involved with more mature businesses, which are those that have a more established historical revenue and profit trend. While these prospect companies have a known track record (which will tend to lower the comparable risk factor versus a start-up, for example), the ROI requirements are still probably going to be similar to those more risky investments. Therefore, while an existing business with a financial track record may slightly lessen the risk influence in the pricing model versus an early-stage investment, private equity firms' ROI requirements and lack of industry synergies will tend to cause them to price their investments higher than VCs would, but below a strategic buyer's price.

Either way, most financial buyers/investors buy a business without ever becoming completely vested in running the operation. They may appreciate your vision, but they may only see your vision as a vehicle for getting what they want—and what they want is to maximize their profit. Don't take it personally. Venture capital and private equity companies acquire equity positions in businesses almost like inventory, and they generally hold them in their portfolios for only three to seven years. As inventory, you are always for sale, with them as investors in your business. These investors do, however, provide valuable funding to targeted companies that fit their industry niche. The idea here is that the purchased company will benefit financially from the investors' expertise, contacts, and positioning. And that very often is the case.

An often-held belief is that financial investors generally do not attempt to work with the existing management team to achieve their mutual goals but rather toss them aside and replace them with their own team. In my experiences I have not found that to be true at all. In fact, a strong management team is often a major consideration in their acquisition because they want to direct the company rather than be hands-on owners.

The returns that VCs and private equity investors earn generally come in two forms: (1) a management-type fee that the acquired company regularly pays to them, and (2) funds on the exit or sale side of the transaction, at which time their original investment is sold off as a whole or in reconfigured pieces.

When you run your business every day like it's for sale, it's important to know what type of buyer you are trying to reach because, as you now know, they are most certainly not all created equally.

Establishing value in the world of financial buyers is primarily a numbers play. Their motivation is driven by their acquisition costs today versus what they believe the value will be at some point in the future—their projected ROI. Their general approach is to garner the highest ownership percentage possible for the least amount of investment so that at the end of their tenured involvement, the value of the investment has been maximized. Although the formula may sound simple and in concept it really is, in practice financial buyers employ a very complex analytical strategy.

Comparatively speaking, financial buyers are generally going to pay less for the same business than would strategic buyers, whose motivation is the acquisition of a product or service that meshes with their existing business model. The strategic buyer is thinking along these lines: "I know my internal metrics will increase with the purchase of the business in question because of the consolidation and/or elimination of overhead in some areas, so my ROI allows me to perhaps pay a slightly higher price."

From My Experience
Buyer Profiles

While working as the chief financial officer (CFO) for United GreenMark, a large West Coast wholesale distributor of irrigation products, I saw firsthand both financial and strategic buyouts. The company had twelve locations in California at the time I came on board. Its owners were openly in the growth-by-acquisition mode. Therefore, over the course of the next two years, the company expanded its footprint by making strategic acquisitions of other irrigation distributors in Arizona, New Mexico, and Nevada, ultimately doubling the number of outlets!

Along the way, the company had created a culture within the organization that nurtured strong employee loyalty and was attractive to high-performing new employees; as you will see, this proactive approach within an organization is #7 in our Ring$ of Value. United GreenMark's entrepreneurial drive to expand the operation by replicating distribution sites and systems to gain market share is a classic example of our Ring #2.

Enter the financial buyer, a private equity group. As it turned out, the successful expansion of our distribution network drew the attention of an East Coast investment firm. It was clear to them that our company had built a level of value that most of our competitors could never match, and so they bought 100 percent of United GreenMark.

Working for a private equity–owned company was like riding on Mr. Toad's Wild Ride at Disneyland. It was filled with quick whipsaw turns and many unexpected ups and downs. A calm run-of-the-mill operation wasn't at the top of their priority list; maximizing their investment was. Those of us operating the company were kept continually apprised of their short-term goals, which were made very, very clear: Raise revenues, lower expenses, and realize more profits. Yes, it was a wild ride, but the learning experience was invaluable.

After five years as an integral part of the private equity group's financial fund, United GreenMark was sold off to John Deere Landscapes (a division of John Deere). John Deere was looking for a West Coast distribution company to complete its coast-to-coast irrigation network concept, and we were the perfect fit!

P.S. Yes, this group did very well financially on the exit.

Valuation through a Buyer's Eyes

This is a topic that I will cover in more detail throughout the book, but I want to introduce the concept here and pose these questions: How *would you* arrive at your company's valuation? Now how *would your prospective buyer* arrive at your valuation? I am pretty sure the two ways will produce very different amounts . . . so together let's understand the *right* way.

Proper valuation of your business is more of an art than a science. Therefore, seeing your business as a potential investor would will help you move above your current role as an owner running the day-to-day operations. This new, broader perspective will provide you with a view beyond the existing enterprise and allow the creation of a working model that truly maximizes its valuation potential.

If you are new to this valuation process, start with your income statement. If you don't know how to really read and interpret one, I encourage you to learn. Such knowledge is key for you as a business owner, not only to run your business but to ultimately help drive your valuation.

Also, **NEVER, NEVER, NEVER** make this statement: "My CPA (or accountant) handles that end of things." It's okay to delegate the preparation of your income tax returns to a CPA (heck, I have a CPA prepare mine *and I am a CPA*), but it is vital for you to know what drives your business tax liabilities. Beyond that, it is invaluable that you understand the impact those tax decisions have on your business's valuation. Therefore, delegate the tax preparation process, but it is imperative that you do **NOT** delegate the knowledge. This again is a point I will stress throughout these pages: Delegate, but never turn a blind eye to any aspect of your business.

The Art and Science of Business Valuation

While there are many models, methods, and theories (e.g., the income, market, or asset-based approaches) on how to value a business from all types of experts, I want you to become fluent in **just one.** So, throughout this book I will help you become so comfortable with this one relatively simple formula that you'll be able to do your own thumbnail valuation of a business at a moment's notice—**just like the Sharks do on *Shark Tank*.** Plus, understanding the formula will provide you with the keys to **unlock the secret method** used by many business brokers in their valuation.

Let me explain more about the art and science of business valuation. Regardless of the method they use, each expert will have his or her own unique jargon and come up with varying dollar valuation ranges depending on the model used and other influences (e.g., company, industry, economic environment, and risks) factored into the calculation. Don't be confused by their attempts to confuse you. I am giving you a formula that will calculate a company's value in about the time it takes to snap your fingers. **But be careful here.** This formula is not an exact science. It is meant to be a quick way to get a *ballpark* number for your business value and is not meant to be a replacement for a truly independent valuation of the business, if needed. Rather, this calculation will give you an approximation of value before you spend a lot of money having a professional appraisal done. On a higher level, understanding this formula will also introduce you to a way of thinking and talking about valuation that is likely new to you, and that understanding will provide you with the decision-making levers to help drive your company to values you never dreamed of before!

So here we go, the single valuation formula for you to learn is:

Value = Profit x a Multiplier + Your Equity, or simply:

$$V = P \times M + E$$

In layman's terms, and assuming no duplication of revenue-producing assets in the calculation, you can quickly arrive at an approximate value (V) for your business by multiplying your adjusted pre-tax profits (P) by your specific industry's standard multiplier (M) and then adding your tangible book equity amount (E).

That's it; that is the entire formula!

And so, given the right buyer, you could sell your company for that "V" amount.

To complete this introduction, let's use our new business formula in a very limited example:

Assume your company's annual adjusted pre-tax profits are $100,000. Your industry's standard multiplier is two, and your tangible book equity is $300,000. In this instance, V = $100,000 x 2 + $300,000 = $500,000.

See how fast the valuation calculation can be?

That simple calculation will provide you with a quick approximation of value for that business. It's extremely useful information that you can calculate extremely fast!

In the normal course of events, this is the price tag a business broker may put on your company. However, know this: It is within your control as a business owner to do better than the industry standard multiplier—much, much better!

We will explore in more depth *how* to know your financial statements inside and out in Chapter 6, but the above example is *why* you need that knowledge. When you can quickly grab values for pre-tax profits and tangible book equity, you have all the ingredients you need to know your company's value. Further, understanding the standard multiplier at work in your particular industry unlocks the key to increasing your value. By using the tools in this book, your index multiplier increases while your peers' multiplier stays stagnant.

We're not done with the study of our formula yet, but for right now here is what I would like you to understand going forward. Some people will imply that the business owner has no control over the industry standard multiplier (M). I am not one of those people. The core concept of the Ring$ of Value is built upon the premise that there are a number of very specific activities that will in fact increase the multiplier that you will be able to apply to your business if and when you decide to sell it or seek outside funding of any kind.

Really Understanding V = P x M + E

As business owners, we tend to think in narrow performance terms: cash in the bank, balance sheets, income statements, and bottom line. In a lot of ways, that's how we guide our businesses. However, in the world of business valuations, the value of your business is only partly driven by these components.

Economists, brokers, and analysts who trumpet exclusive expertise will assign a generic industry multiplier that may or may not be valid to your specific business. Nonetheless, the multiplier, which is an accumulation of thoughts, metrics, and risks in your particular industry, can be difficult to manipulate if you don't have the right tools.

Those right tools are not some illusive, amorphous concept open to but a select few. They are meant for anyone who understands that leadership is not about lighting a fire under people, it's about lighting a fire inside them. They are tools that demonstrate to your employees, your stakeholders, your vendors, and your customers that you see leadership as a way of maximizing your business's day-to-day performance while traveling well beyond the noise.

Put simply, you're not stuck with the same M value that others may try to assign to you or that your peers are using. Your multiplier could be numerically enhanced by any or all of our Ring$ of Value: Cultural Environment, Innovation, Revenue Streams, Distribution Channels, Branding and Public Identification, Ability to Replicate and Scale, and Power to Change Lives. By actively engaging inside your Ring$ of Value, you can and will claim control over your company's valuation formula rather than simply accepting a formula set by your industry norm.

Bottom line, I don't want you to settle for average when you are selling the business that you poured your heart and soul into!

Future versus Past

Within our valuation formula are actually two factors that you can control and thus change. The future consists of both P and M because any changes made can proactively impact both the profit and the multiplier. Experts generally refer to the

P x M portion of the formula as the value that is being assigned to the business operation itself. In other words, going forward what value do these experts project the operations to generate? The past is your existing E, equity, or whatever profits have been retained in the business. Although the E will change with the company's performance, at the moment a valuation calculation is done it is unchangeable because it is your historical result. Alas, we can never change the past.

Clearly, the ability **to add value** is vital to the M (multiplier) factor that potential buyers or investors will use in evaluating the value of your operation. But keep this very important idea top of mind: As powerful as the knowledge of our seven Rings and this valuation formula are, productive engagement within one or more of the Ring$ of Value inevitably creates a company that is performing financially better too. Better financial performance equals increased adjusted profits. Therefore, while your M is increasing from your Ring$ of Value activities, you will most likely see a simultaneous improvement in your P factor of our formula as well as the M for a **double-valuation win!**

Adjusted Profits, aka Alphabet Soup

Let's start by breaking down the formula $V = P \times M + E$. Digging more deeply into adjusted profits, the P in our formula, it's important to know how experienced buyers arrive at their calculated amount. This becomes especially pertinent when a suitor is comparing two different enterprises; adjusted profits require some standardization across the income statements to get a fair "apples to apples" comparison. To accomplish this standardization, most multiple-approach valuations are calculated using EBITDA as their starting point for adjusted profits. Say what? No, EBITDA is not a mysterious virus. It is an acronym that stands for earnings before interest, (income) taxes, depreciation, and amortization. EBITDA calculates what business analysts refer to as free cash flow, or a level of profit *before* all the above-mentioned expenses.

We all remember the saying "Cash is king." Well, in business valuations, this old adage is still very, very relevant. Free cash flow is another way of measuring how much cash the business will generate. To experienced buyers or investors, business valuation can come down to one word: *risk*. In their minds, a higher P in the formula equals a higher resulting free cash flow, which lowers their risk—and most important of all increases your sales price! That's why having cash is king. And, just to be clear, the opposite is true as well. That is, if P is low, cash flow is low, so the perceived risk is high and the valuation amount is lowered.

To further the definition of our P value, we start with EBITDA and then tweak it even more by adding or subtracting the following adjustments. These adjustments can be *one-time changes* or *ongoing costs* that temper the future revenue and expense trend a buyer would expect to realize. By modifying an existing EBITDA with these adjustments, buyers are attempting to normalize what they expect the revenue and expense stream will be for them. They're trying to figure out what they can expect their future free cash flow will be in order to calculate their ROI. This calculation helps them see what true profitability run rate they will realize. **That is why P is referred to as *adjusted* profits in our formula.**

Your EBITDA value is very much derived from your income statement. In fact, some more advanced business income statements actually show this key number as a subtotal before net income. You might consider trying to calculate the current P of your business as it is today. Here's how: After you get your income statement from your CPA, you first calculate your existing EBITDA (if it is not already evident) and then make the adjustments a buyer would make (e.g., for excess owner compensation, personal expenses running through the business, one-time revenue bumps, etc.). The result from that exercise will be your very important adjusted P. We will get into more examples throughout the book to help you get even more comfortable with this key calculation.

A company's EBITDA and any resulting adjustments combine to equal adjusted profits, which are also sometimes referred to as pro forma profits or the pro forma income statement for the buyer. A pro forma income statement is simply the investors' projection of an expected/normalized run rate *if* they were to purchase the business. **Please note:** The academic definition of *pro forma income statement* is one that adjusts out extraordinary (e.g., lawsuit costs and settlement) and nonrecurring items (e.g., a one-time inventory write-down or a one-time significant sale), and then normalizes the expenses to reflect what a hypothetical buyer would realize (e.g., any adjustments to key executive compensation and benefits to the level that matches the buyer's business model). In a later chapter we will go into some numerical examples, but for now the concept is most important.

So why is this important, why is it even an issue? When all you are trying to do is to get an idea of the value your company, what difference does all this jargon even make? Well, I am not sure who made the rules, and while they may seem counterintuitive (for example, why would we leave expenses out of a valuation formula?) **these ARE the rules**.

Think of adjusted profits as a standardizing measuring point. Since every business has its own unique debt structure, varying income tax strategies and expenses, asset capitalization amounts and policies, and origination costs, when calculating any company's value, the professionals leave out (though they actually call it "add-back") these items in a business valuation. This is because a potential buyer doesn't give a hoot about the amounts you paid on such line-item expenses, because their expense run rates are going to be very different from yours.

Multipliers Explained

Every industry has its particular multiple based on investor risk tolerance; brokers will tell you this factor ebbs and flows with market conditions, ROI, regions, and the current economy. Typically, smaller businesses will sell in a one- to five-times M multiple range, while larger companies can realize double-digit multiples. Now these are fairly wide ranges, so let's look at how to determine what applies to your particular industry.

If *you* are the business, as in it's a sole proprietorship, then you are going to be on the lower end of the range, perhaps a one- or two-times multiplier or lower. This is because a buyer factors in a higher level of risk associated with a one-person show. If you are a dentist, physical therapist, or consultant without partners, for example, you fall into this category. If you own a stand-alone coffee shop or cafe where either your name is attached to the business or everyone associates you, your face, as well as your reputation with the business, then again the business will have lower multiples because the perception is that this enterprise is more vulnerable because it consists of a single person or single location versus a company with broader name identification or more locations. The reason for the reduced multiples is that a new buyer knows he or she will have to overcome this identification bias, thus their perceived risk of investment is higher and so their projected ROI is reduced. A reduced ROI equals a reduced multiplier factor.

On the other hand, businesses that have multiple owners and/ or locations and have a strong historical pattern of sales and profit growth, repeat customers, and more than a few years of good standing in business will generally garner a lower level of risk to an investor. This, in turn, equates to a higher perceived ROI and therefore may move to a three- to five-times multiplier, or more!

If you have a proprietary concept, either a product or service, or other characteristics that distinguish you from your industry peers, if you own an exclusive sales or service territory, or if your business happens to be in a growing industry, your company multiplier will likely be at the higher end of the range and *may be* beyond!

—————

Generally speaking, the higher the risk involved in a company's operations or the industry they are active in, the lower the multiplier, and vice versa: the lower the perceived risk, the higher the multiple.

—————

However, risk, like beauty, is in the eye of the beholder. One person's risk may not be another's. And risk doesn't always look numerical, either. For example, a maturing industry or product line may have good performing historical financials, but a buyer may lower the valuation multiple because he or she may not interpret the future to be as bright.

In service industries that produce residual income or have extremely strong customer loyalty, say an insurance company, a medical practice, or the veterinary example I used earlier, the M can range from two to as high as double digits (in rare circumstances). Think about that. For every dollar P increases, V goes up two to ten dollars! In dollars and cents this means a $100,000 improvement in P = $200,000 if your M is two, or up to a whopping $1,000,000 increase to V if you have a ten-times multiplier!

Rest assured, if you have an eight- to ten-times multiplier, you are doing things right. Furthermore, chances are good that you are engaging in one or more of the Ring$ of Value, even if you did not recognize it before.

Finding Your M

To find the industry standard multiplier that typically governs the market in which your company operates, you can take a number of simple steps. Call a qualified business broker specializing in your core area (understanding that not all business brokers are created equal). Check trade publications and compare any published transaction data on businesses in your industry. Search the internet for valuation sites or services. Or, reach out to owners of similarly sized companies in your industry who have been through the sale process, if they are open to it.

Know this: There are only two types of businesses, product-based and service-based. You're either selling a product or selling a service. So, for comparison's sake, make sure the companies you benchmark occupy the same space in the market or work in the same industry as you. Then, if you find a company that recently sold for more than market value, you've more than likely stumbled upon a company with experience in our Ring$ of Value model. It's like the house that outsells its comparable counterparts because the owners have always held their property to higher standards.

You may be asking, "Why do I care?"

Here's why: Knowing how to find your company's M (multiplier) in our formula is a key to this question: "How much can I realistically sell my business for?"

If you are a small or medium-sized company, it is likely that you will have to answer this question for yourself. Having a professional valuation calculated can be too cost-prohibitive, unless you are in fact putting your company on the market. As well, your CPA very likely won't have the correct metrics and formulas to help you determine these values, since their main task is ensuring that the numbers on your balance sheet and income statement all fall into place and that the taxes you are paying are correct. Yes, your CPA can and should help you ferret out any and all tax deductions applicable to you and your operation. Yes, he or she can and should help you with thoughts on how to reduce certain expenses, apply tax strategies, and analyze cash flow, but for this calculation, CPAs are subject to exposure issues beyond their specialty and so they will more than likely refer you to a valuation professional.

But don't fret. With the tools and understanding of our formula, it's very doable for you to be able to get a very good estimate of your market value **without incurring the costs of an outside opinion**!

E is for Equity

The E in our formula is really defined as the company's tangible net worth, or TNW, which is a calculation of a company's value *without* intangible assets. So Assets - Intangible Assets - Liabilities = TNW. I know . . . ugh! If you have a rock star CPA, you might find that this number is already on your balance sheet. For most companies, TNW is essentially their stockholder equity amount. Usually it is a number clearly identified on the balance sheet as total equity or stockholder's equity. However, just to be clear on a very key point, it is essential when using this valuation formula that you do not double count any revenue-producing assets. Therefore, when adding your E at the end of the formula, just be certain not to have already assumed any of those same assets into the P x M portion of your calculation. So, for simplicity of the formula and the examples throughout this book, let's just assume that E is your stockholder equity and the number does not include any duplication of revenue-producing assets. For you number hounds, we actually do an exercise in Chapter 9 that shows how this entire equity calculation breaks down so you *can* learn to do it yourself!

I am aware that these technical explanations can make your eyes glaze over with tedium. Maybe this will help: Think of the E in this formula as a **valuation kicker**. You see, once you have calculated the value for the continuing operations of the business (P x M), the amount of E is then ADDED on! A cherry on top, in a manner of speaking. If your E is a big number, then you have a bigger cherry than others.

A side note: Your "sweat equity" is different from this tangible equity (E), but it's also valuable to you. As a business owner, always be conscious of how much time and money you have invested in your business versus how much it is worth. These opportunity costs (for example, any forfeited options for higher compensation or for your finite time) need to be monitored to make sure that they are less than the actual value of your company. In fact, you want that difference to be as large as possible.

What Is Your Business Really Worth?

Whether you are entertaining the idea of selling some ownership in your company or pitching a full sale to a potential buyer, you should do so with an educated estimate of the value of your business in mind. Ultimately, the buy/sell process is a negotiation between the buyer's perceived or calculated value and the seller's. The crucial question in every one of these negotiating conversations is, are your valuation numbers similar to a prospective investor's calculated result? In other words, do you have a mutual starting point to negotiate from? These potential investors will study your balance sheet and income statement, but their questions will probe much deeper than that.

They will ask whether or not you're taking a salary. In fact, this is a biggie. If company owners aren't paying themselves or are purposefully underpaying themselves in an attempt to artificially increase the bottom line, then the P in our formula, the profit, is higher than it should be. After deducting a reasonable salary for someone to run the daily business (which an investor will factor into the calculation), maybe it suddenly becomes a much less enticing or valuable investment.

They will ask if your business is a product-based business, and if so, if you own the patents or intellectual property (IP) for this product. This is a question about innovation (Ring #6). If anyone can duplicate your invention after seeing an article about it in *Businessweek* or if all your competitors are doing the same thing, it's obviously not as valuable as you may have purported.

You will be asked who else is invested in your company. This can be either a positive or a negative to potential new investors. Even if this information doesn't directly impact their valuation of your business, it will influence their decision on whether they want to be involved with these other partners.

You may be asked whether you have scaled your product or services to broader markets or whether you have only had success in your immediate market.

You may have to field any number of financial questions, such as: How are your sales tracking to your projections? What are your operating profit margins? Certainly having ready answers will build confidence with the people asking the questions, but are your answers the right answers?

At the root of every query is the all-important question that is the impetus for this book: **What is your business really worth?**

As I am sure you can sense by now, once a negotiation begins, the opportunities to *reduce* your overall value are plentiful, but there are just as many ways to *increase that value* too, so stay with me! This is where the Rings of Value enter the picture and the evolution of your business into something wildly valuable begins.

Chapter 2 Takeaways

1. Knowing the valuation formula V = P x M + E is an extremely powerful tool for you to quickly calculate your business's worth at any moment, given a willing buyer.

2. When calculating P, or your adjusted profits, leave out your debt interest, income taxes, depreciation, and amortization expenses (also known as EBITDA) because that is exactly what an experienced buyer or investor will do.

3. Despite what advisors might tell you, you *can* influence the M (multiplier) in your business valuation formula by engaging in the Rings of Value!

CHAPTER 3

APPLYING V = P X M + E

O nce you understand the basics of adjusted profits, here is a fun and interesting "what-if" exercise you can do: As you start tinkering with factors that impact your profit, your valuation also changes. For example, an expense reduction that improves your P will have an exponential impact on V, because your M will now be multiplying a higher P. So now, as you look for ways to improve your processing or operating costs, those reductions are suddenly far more valuable to you than just the face value of the original reduction. With this knowledge, you will never look at expense reductions in the same way again. Try it!

Let's say you own a bakery and your valuation multiplier for your business is a two. Further, let's assume it costs you $2.00 to make a loaf of bread, and you sell each loaf for $5.00. Thinking like most business owners do, for every loaf of bread you sell, you are making a profit of $3.00. Say you sell 10,000 loaves a month. That is a gross profit of $30,000/month (10,000 loaves x $3.00 gross profit), or $360,000/year. Yay for profits!

Now let's look at what happens from the adjusted profits/valuation formula perspective if there is a positive change in the cost of goods sold for the bread.

Maybe you get a sweet new volume deal on flour, or you reengineer your recipe to require fewer of the mostly costly ingredients while still maintaining that yummy taste. All these factors lower your costs from $2.00 per loaf to $1.50 per loaf. So while it is just $0.50 lower in per-loaf production costs, that is a $0.50 higher gross profit per loaf. Seem small? Well at those volumes, that $0.50 per loaf equates to $5,000 (10,000 loaves x $0.50) more in gross profit margin per month, which then extrapolates out to a $60,000 increase per year ($5,000 x 12) for just changing the cost structure. Pretty darn good, right? Yes it is, but there's more!

If you, our baker, can show a potential investor or buyer that these cost reductions can be realized without any dip in revenues, then you could extrapolate or project out these results in an adjusted profits calculation to pro forma these results for valuation purposes. Then, by applying our valuation formula to that same increased calculated profit margin, whatever your bakery company was worth just increased in value by the reduction in expenses times their multiple of two, or $120,000 ($60,000 x 2)!

We are not dealing from the bottom of the deck here, either. If you can prove to your potential buyers that your operating costs are really lower and therefore your P will project higher, then your company's value goes up by those cost savings times your multiple. So not only did you increase the bakery's pre-tax profits by $60,000, you also concurrently increased the business value by $120,000 for an overall increase of $180,000 ($60,000 + $120,000). Or think about this way: A cost improvement of just $0.50 per loaf extends to a whopping $180,000 more in combined personal worth!

Behold, the power of these simple mathematics!

Since the math gets easier and quicker the more comfortable you are with the valuation formula, let's continue this what-if scenario. Let's say your bakery, in addition to the above gross profit improvement, reduces its annual payroll by $25,000. So again, if you can prove to a potential buyer that going forward the bakery will indeed realize an additional $25,000 in expense reductions so that its annual profits will then be $25,000 higher, then the bakery valuation just went up an additional $50,000 ($25,000 x 2). Oh, and don't forget, the overall personal pre-tax worth increased another $75,000 ($25,000 from the improved profits + $50,000 in increased business valuation). Best of all, this valuation increase can be passed along to your potential buyer or investor whether the $25,000 is actually realized or just presented on a solid projection, if it can be verified.

But hold on, if we combine both the $0.50 per loaf cost improvement with the $25,000 payroll reduction, your bakery's overall pre-tax net worth just went up $180,000 + $75,000, or $255,000. The right potential investor or buyer will pay this higher amount because you have proven that your bakery is that much more valuable!

That is the numerical power of the V = P x M + E formula at work.

It is, however, worth emphasizing here that many businesses do concentrate too much on cutting costs at the expense of strategic increases. This occurs across industries, from the corner bakery to the Fortune 500 companies that lay workers off every time they miss their quarterly stock projections. There is a time and a place for reducing expenses. Reducing expenses when it does not infringe on product integrity or customer satisfaction can be good policy, but I am known for evangelizing on this point: **In the long run, you can't cut your way to success.**

A Better Way

Beyond good business-process improvement and expense monitoring, an additional way to jump to even higher business valuations is to enhance your existing business model with the Ring$ of Value. Let's look at how that might play out.

Say your bakery's bread is extra special in some way . . . maybe it's gluten-free while maintaining a soft, chewy texture. Every gluten-intolerant customer in your market knows about your amazing gluten-free bread and drives across town to buy it. Now your bakery has employed a higher level of innovation, which is represented in the sixth of our value Rings.

According to our Rings of Value formula, $V = P \times M + E$, M is numerically increased by any and all of the seven Rings. In this instance, it's Ring #6, Innovation. So the bottom line is that your bakery's valuation will calculate even higher than its competitors, not because you cut corners or trimmed your workforce, but because you engaged the Rings of Value and implemented a long-term value-enhancing strategy. Buyers and investors recognize the value-add that any of the Rings have on M and will pay more for these companies!

Caution: M diminishers (Yes, M can go up or down . . .)

This book's premise is built on the idea that there are **M (multiplier) enhancers** such as creating a desirable cultural environment, innovation in your industry, or building brand awareness. But while M can giveth, it can also taketh away. There are indeed **M (multiplier) diminishers**, so proceed with caution.

M diminishers are really the alter ego of the positive Rings. Examples include:

• Employee culture and/or management team that is perceived to be worse than the industry standard

• A loss of brand identity, or an incident that damages your company's reputation

• Stagnancy in innovation, or failed product lines

• Revenue streams that are drying up or experiencing market share encroachment

• Closures of satellite locations if they are perceived as retrenchment

Valuation Price Adjustments

One particularly costly valuation diminisher is the dreaded price adjustment. These are sales price reductions, or dollar for dollar adjustments. A more familiar example of this might be when you are selling a house and opt to include a carpet or roof allowance to close the deal. Similarly, a business valuation adjustment could include a reserve for pending litigation settlement or an allowance for excessive or poor quality inventory.

Sometimes in valuation adjustments, the purpose of the transaction comes into play. For instance, think succession planning in a family company versus a financial buyer purchase. Or if this buyer is purchasing more or less than a controlling interest, that will impact the price. For example, if the sale is for less than a controlling interest (also called a minority purchase), then there is usually a pricing discount because of the lack of decision-making control this ownership position has. There can also be a marketability liquidity discount if the buyer has resale restrictions on their minority ownership.

Terms of the deal also directly impact the pricing of a transaction. If a seller will take payment terms from the buyer or will be agreeable to an "earn out" formula, where the price is adjustable based on the future performance (usually for two to five years) of the business up or down, that could produce a higher pricing model.

The key point here is that all of the above WILL impact the final transaction price.

How Your Buyer Will View Your Valuation

Imagine a conversation with a potential buyer who is really looking at your entire business model. He or she is asking you the tough questions to really get a sense of everything in play. You can expect queries like this:

Buyer: How about your product line? What about that widget you've been selling forever. Is it still one of your mainstays?

You: Well, it's been in our product line since the beginning. It's still a good product. One of our mainstays? Well, I don't know if I'd call it that . . .

Buyer Thinks: Well, that's a demerit because you don't even know the future market viability of your longest-standing product.

Buyer: Do you have any litigation pending against your business right now?

You: Well, there's this one. It's kind of simmering. It's not really doing anything as the moment, but . . .

Buyer Thinks: Here comes a valuation deduction.

Buyer: What does your inventory look like?

You: Well, my inventory looks really good.

Buyer: Okay, what do you mean by good? That everything in stock is salable? Is that what you're telling me? Everything is current and salable?

You: Well, no, I didn't say that . . .

Buyer Thinks: Inventory write-downs are like taking candy from a baby and very, very easy valuation price reduction targets!

All of a sudden, that business isn't worth as much because your product lines don't have the sizzle to someone else that you think they do, or you've failed to mention a potential legal issue, or you've overstated your inventory. Those imps lurking in the back room may not show up as liabilities on your balance sheet, but you probably know they are there. They are the issues that keep you up at night. My advice? Treat them as if you're selling your business tomorrow. Fix them before they cost you real valuation money, *because if you were the buyer, you wouldn't want them either— would you?* Treat the buyer with the same respect that you would want if the roles were reversed.

Your buyer will be paying as much attention to the M diminishers within your business as he or she will the M enhancers. You should too.

When you are making your list of possible M diminishers, always, always, always pay special attention to the following owner/ operator blind spots:

- Product line liability
- Litigation issues
- Excess inventory
- Market share encroachment
- Underperforming employees

Just like when you're selling your house, any potential buyer or investor will be looking at the bones of your business. Instead of foundations, roofs, and insulation, we're talking about inventory, management teams, and customer loyalty. So, while it's worth the time to make sure the surface-level business is sparkling and attractive, know that your enterprise's biggest assets are found at its core.

Catching a Buyer's Attention

What is it, then, that will truly catch a buyer's attention above and beyond cleaning up your income statement and balance sheet—what I refer to as good business hygiene? The answer is your active engagement within the Ring$ of Value. You could be selling bottled water, running a landscaping company, or starting up an internet marketing firm, but the message is the same: Think first and foremost about what a buyer is going to want from your business. As long as it makes sense in your business plan, then consider which Ring$ of Value can best advance the components within the formula V = P x M + E.

Aiming for another deduction on your tax return is not how you build wealth. Nobody cares about the money you paid on your tax returns except you and your accountant. The same applies to the use of high-ticket advisors just for the sake of name recognition.

From My Experience
Beware of Designer Advisors

I once worked as a consultant to a real estate development company that used a pricey CPA firm for their professional accounting and tax needs. Their hourly rates ranged from $500 per hour to $2,000 per hour for their "experienced advice." I was hired as a link between the company's ownership and its CPAs. For all the power and name recognition of the CPA firm, I was the one who located a major liability (a contingent lawsuit), potentially costing thousands of dollars, that any qualified buyer or investor would immediately see as a red flag, a valuation deduction, and an integrity black eye. This kind of juicy valuation diminisher for a buyer may not be the kind of thing you find in obvious places like on a balance sheet; rather, it's the kind of thing that happens "between" the sheets. The point here is to make sure that whatever it is, that you find it and properly deal with it before it becomes an issue to your buyer.

The lesson is this: Many business owners think hiring a certain level of consultants is a panacea. It's not true. Just because you pay a third party a bunch of fees for advice doesn't mean you have increased the real value of your business. The same is true of your legal team. Getting legal advice on some labor dispute or intellectual property matter doesn't mean you have upped the V in our formula. Those services are in the business noise category, and in many ways sap your innovation and creativity. Those services are nothing positive to a potential buyer. In fact, the noise may distract them.

Most potential buyers and investors view time as one of their most precious assets. When they approach prospects about their businesses, the most attractive ventures in their eyes are going to be the ones with owners who have already done the hard work and have taken steps toward the more advanced valuation that can be realized within the Ring$ of Value. Those businesses with a desirable cultural environment, innovative products and services, established distribution channels, and recognizable brand identity will integrate quickly and require little or no reorganization. These are the businesses that buyers are most interested in putting their money into. **The target you should aim your business and your energies toward are the Ring$ of Value.**

Chapter 3 Takeaways

1. Have some fun by tinkering with your own what-if valuation scenarios. What if you cut that extraneous staff position? What if you opened a new branch? How much would your business be worth if you made this change or that?

2. Don't be blind to M diminishers; fix them before they cost you real valuation dollars.

3. Look at your own business as if you were going to buy it, and be brutally honest about your flaws or any questionable items. Then correct them so that you realize the financial reward, not your buyer!

CHAPTER 4

THE RING$ OF VALUE

I hope I have impressed upon you the enormous potential for value enhancement through expanded effort in the Ring$ of Value. Visualizing our valuation formula, V = P x M + E, you will remember P as the day-to-day activities and the results from running your business. Again, P is your adjusted profit from your income statement (plus or minus valuation add-backs and/or adjustments). Or better yet, P is your effort to raise revenues while controlling costs; it is monitoring your position relative to your industry and using your metrics to track performance and growth. Once those essentials are mastered, you can graduate to working on your M (multiplier). **You can see now that you have to earn your way through understanding your business**. Then, when you have done that, like walking into the Land of Oz, you get to see your business in full color.

The Ring$ of Value are the elements that increase your M, which is what buyers and investors are keenly interested in. If properly demonstrated, these same parties can be so interested in your Rings' activities that they will pay an increased V for your business because you have clearly separated yourself from your peers.

Unfortunately, there isn't a tangible calculation I can give you to show exactly how much more valuable your organization will be because of the impact of each Ring; it is relative to each specific business and industry. **But rest assured that your overall value will go up—exponentially.** So, when a potential buyer/investor/ stakeholder looks at your business and sees you are engaged in the Rings, the M for your company will be greater than your competitors' M because they are just going about their business in the day-to-day noise.

The reason that these Rings **can add so much market value so quickly** is because of the simple mathematics from the compounding effects. These Rings are actually adding incremental volume, revenue, and therefore value to your business or division. The concept *incremental* is key because your current overhead costs are, for the most part, already being covered by the core business. Adding layers or Rings on top of your existing enterprise is the mathematical magic to the exponential value drivers. So incremental revenues = much higher contribution margins coming from these added-on activities. Higher contribution margins = higher P for profits, and your M (multiplier) also rises because of this extra Ring factor. A double WIN!

Visually, I have laid the Rings out in an order that my expertise has shown they impact M, from the least but still impactful outer Ring to the highest impact Ring, the center of the target. However, the order of value enhancements is not set in stone. Regardless of the order, the most important point is that each Ring can ADD to M, which INCREMENTALLY ADDS to your V.

As you start to take aim at the target, keep in mind that your active participation in the Ring$ of Value will be reflected in a suitor's view of how valuable your company is relative to your industry peers. Some companies only invest in one Ring, while others have several Rings spinning simultaneously. What is your appetite?

Let's now examine even more closely each value-enhancing Ring. From the outside Ring to the target center, we start with:

Ring #7: Cultural Environment

This Ring holds everything else in place. Your company's culture is a mix of your core values and those of your employees. Since they are the glue that binds your company together *and* the face of your business in the public, taking care in choosing your team is paramount.

Talented employees don't just appear; they are drawn to dynamic environments. That magnetic pull is the second benefit of a positive cultural environment. A magnetic company is one where people want to be—think Apple and Facebook. Those are the big names, but hundreds of lesser-known companies also make their respective "Best Places to Work" lists. These are enterprises where devoted employees love to contribute.

By magnetism, I don't mean there are foosball tables in the break room.

Yes, modern companies do need to understand that younger generations want to structure their work/life balance differently, but more than that, successful companies understand that their staff want to spend their time doing something meaningful. As an example, consider one of the internet's most-used websites: Wikipedia. Why do so many talented people spend their free time building content for zero remuneration? Founder Jimmy Wales answers, "Because it's awesome." His perfunctory response notwithstanding, Wales understands the intangible "it factor" very well. He has created a site that people are proud to contribute to—for free! Successful companies become awesome because they allow employees to embrace a mission, to be a part of creating something new and exciting.

From My Experience
The Pied Piper

My first job after I left public accounting was with a company called Willitts Designs. In its inception, the company distributed decorative bath soaps and accessories. But the company's second CEO, Bill Willitts, was an innovator. Once in control, he moved out of those maturing product lines and expanded into the design and import of high-end gift and collectibles items. He courted and secured lucrative product licensing deals with Charles Schultz for his Peanuts characters. He also added Disney licenses for Winnie the Pooh and many others. Through his leadership style, Bill lured talented artists and designers from all over. He just knew the importance of bringing quality items to the market at a price point that customers could afford. Ultimately, through Bill's vision and leadership, Willitts Designs was sold to Hallmark Cards.

There was something about Bill that drew people to him, which is why I thought of him as a modern-day Pied Piper. You know the type, those special people in our lives and businesses who are just enjoyable to be around. Bill was unequivocally the company president, but his business cards listed the unassuming title "Coach." Bill preferred to see himself as more of a teacher than a boss. And he *never* considered himself as above the next person. The combination of his magnetic personality, humility, and business creativity developed and cultivated an environment that everyone just wanted to be a part of. Those genuine characteristics allowed him to assemble an extremely talented, self-perpetuating team that translated to real synergy in the work environment.

At first glance, Hallmark Cards appeared to be most interested in Willitts Designs for its industry niche and product licenses. However, beyond those obvious reasons, Hallmark's secondary motivation for the acquisition was actually the speed at which Willitts brought new products to market. Our typical product development cycle was about nine months from the concept in the artist's eye through overseas production and distribution to the retailers. At that time, Hallmark's cycle was about two years. So for them, the value of Willitts's cultural environment also translated to a significant cost savings in their development chain and speed of fulfillment. Speed! What a huge potential boost to their bottom line, and this perpetuating benefit would then have a huge continuing impact on Hallmark's own valuation.

The lesson to be learned here is this: Don't try to outthink your buyers, because you may never really know what is motivating them to action and you could negatively impact your transaction by trying to figure it out.

One other word of caution regarding cultural environment beyond your company's magnetic draw: Pay attention to who in your company is doing the new employee recruiting. Sometimes as companies get bigger, recruitment becomes problematic. Talented employees, let's call them A-level employees, recruit other A's, which is a very positive part of the self-perpetuation process. These A-level employees want the challenge and synergy of other top-level talent and, interestingly, are not threatened by it. Rather, they are further energized by the creativity. B-level employees want C-level coworkers for the exact opposite reason. They want someone who will not be a threat to them and their position within the company. So think about it in your organization: Are you hiring A-level employees, or is your team hiring C's?

Attracting talented employees is even more important from the viewpoint of tomorrow. Think who you will need not just for today, but what your needs will be tomorrow. In other words, the people who got you to your current business level are not necessarily the ones you will need to move to the next level of your business. Studies have shown that the cost of hiring the wrong person can be *five to fifteen times* their annual pay, so don't take the recruitment and hiring process for granted. Be involved!

Ring #6: Innovation

Lots and lots of people have ideas, but the key distinction with innovation is the element of action that actually brings those ideas to market. Implementation is the key! Regardless of their size, companies can change, disrupt, and/or dominate their entire industry through innovation. Beyond the obvious boost to top-line sales for a new product or service that hits, there can also be a significant profit margin realized by those who are first in the market. Higher revenues combined with higher profit margins from the early stages of a new idea's life cycle can be a double win to your bottom line!

So if you are in or interested in this Ring, your best energies are spent focusing on the speed of transforming new visions and ideas into something of actual value to the consumer, with the motto that your competitors won't be able to catch you.

As demonstrated in the Willitts Designs example above, **innovation is enhanced by developing a solid cultural environment.** Your confident and dedicated team is what creates an innovation continuum with staying power. Conversely, if your team isn't fully on board with a new product or service, then chances are your customers won't be either.

Understand that I am not expecting you to create the universe overnight. Yes, there are innovators in the marketplace who seem to be idea factories, but they are the exception to the rule. People like Steve Jobs come along once in a generation, and even he had a team of innovators behind him. You also don't have to be a creative genius to be an innovator in your field. Most businesses, maybe even your business, began with one idea—one superior mousetrap that really changed the conversation in that industry. The trick is to avoid becoming a one-hit wonder. So if your one idea made a pretty good splash in the industry some years ago, so what? Without follow-up products, your company could fizzle after a single hit, or two or even three hits. To ensure continued staying power, there must be more and more and more innovation. If that sounds daunting, fear not.

People sometimes forget that all product concepts do not have to be conceived within the company's walls. Product ideas can be purchased or licensed to supplement existing product lines. That is what Willitts Designs did. Beyond the internal design team, the company had complementary gift product lines that were created by outside artists to whom we paid license agreements. These included the Peanuts and Disney characters mentioned in the description of Ring #7. What started out as a bath soap company morphed into this nationally sought-after giftware business because one good idea just sprouted another good idea, and so on.

By reaching out to possible partners, tweaking and improving the existing product lines, and listening to all the voices in your target market and within your own company, new ideas *will* come. Again, new ideas are the fuel that increases this Ring, your multiplier, and thus your overall value. Any potential investor is going to be financially intrigued by innovation.

Sometimes we consumers imagine that innovation only comes from product-based businesses. However, innovation happens just as often in service-based companies. The most common patents granted by the U.S. Patent and Trademark Office are actually utility patents for items with useful processes. Though it's harder to conceptualize because consumers don't drive to the store and buy a process, the ways you make something happen can be just as innovative as a better mousetrap. As an example, the service industry is witnessing a big push toward codifying positive customer interaction by modernizing technologies. It is becoming commonplace for websites to allow customers to set meeting schedules, exchange confidential data, and process orders 24/7. This way companies are making it more convenient for customers to transact business, and the users are getting a more interactive experience that fits their schedule and needs. Remember, it is all about customers and their changing needs, not yours. If your business is in the service industry, don't discount your opportunity to expand value through this Ring because if you don't, someone else will!

Moving inward on the Ring$ of Value, have you ever thought of taking your innovative idea and developing it into an entirely new avenue of business altogether? When you create a brand-new source of income with your idea, you delve into . . .

Ring #5: Revenue Streams

If you want to increase revenues without raising prices, you can either sell more of your existing products or services, or you can add additional revenue streams. In other words, you can diversify. Most of us think of revenue in linear terms: make this product style then that product style, a large version followed by a smaller one. But all product and service concepts don't have to just run north/south or east/west with your existing markets. A new revenue stream (which can simply mean any method that brings additional money into a company) may have you leaving the roads you are currently on completely and jumping to an entirely different track. Consider the way Apple started in computers, morphed into portable electronics such as iPhones, and then started making watches, and who knows from there? Expanding the same products by adding more colors and gadgets is innovation; new product and service categories are new revenue streams.

You don't have to be a Fortune 500 company to diversify into a new line of revenue either. Here are just a few examples from my own career.

United GreenMark was an irrigation products wholesale and distribution company, yet ironically its most profitable division was in the water conservation arena. Its proprietary technology, which controlled the drip systems for municipalities and college campuses, was highly desirable. This division was so valuable that it was almost sold off separately, but ultimately it was an instrumental component in increasing the total value of the sales price of the aggregate company, which was sold to John Deere.

Tuff Stuff Inc. was a publisher of its own baseball card valuation guide. During my tenure there as a senior executive, we branched out into the trading card industry ourselves by developing a Civil War card series as well as an exclusive Peanuts character collector series—a license agreement I negotiated from my prior contacts at Willitts Designs. That was a really fun new revenue stream for Tuff Stuff that also demonstrates a crucial lesson: Never turn your back on any valuable business relationship! You just never know.

Another company I worked with developed high-end commercial real estate. They built trendy office buildings, industrial parks, etc. and ran them as the core business model. As part of this business strategy, they would buy bare land when prices were low and hold it until they had enough corporate tenant interest to build out a building or business park, which could be years. Rather than let the parcels sit empty, leaking money before they could build out the business park, they built golf courses on them to offset the carrying costs. Now that was a clever additional revenue stream!

These examples are very creative ways small to medium-sized companies that I worked with entered into new markets and created additional revenue streams. Don't let your company's size forestall you from trying something similar. The biggest obstacle to entering new revenue streams is stale thinking. We get so stuck in our ruts, driving to work, blasting away at the to-do list all day, then driving the same route home, where we fall into bed. New ideas happen when you step out of your routine. Think about what your business looks like from your customers' perspective. Or how about after you have been away on vacation? Coming back, you see everything differently, with fresh eyes. It is suddenly easier to clear away clutter and begin new projects because you can more easily recognize the minutia.

It's also financially easier than you think to bring a small to medium-sized business into a new revenue stream because, as noted in the beginning of this chapter, much of the overhead for any new diversification could be absorbed by your current line of business. All the necessary overhead, including your pay, is covered by the current profits. For this new revenue source, all you have to do is cover the incremental costs of that new innovation, leaving all the gross profit from this new adventure to drop straight to your bottom line!

Find time to take a step back. Even if you can't spend two weeks away, you *can* get away from your office for think time. You *can* go to an industry conference. You *can* take a webinar at which your peers are sharing ideas and learning about new methods and concepts. The extra energy really is worth the effort—try it. Challenge yourself; **you can think differently**.

Ring #4: Distribution Channels

Just like with revenue streams, you can develop distribution channels as a small to medium business too. First, let's define the term. Distribution channels are well-established logistical networks that move a product or service from the platform to the customer. They enable companies to spread their reach over large geographic regions, like Amazon does. Similar to adding a new revenue stream, adding a distribution channel is a whole new vector in which a company can address its market. For example, consider the way the television model has changed in the last decade.

Instead of looking for shows on specific channels, consumers now stream from various entertainment hosts such as Netflix, Hulu, or HBO Go. So creators have multiple channels for addressing their markets and multiple opportunities to make money from the same show or movie, depending on where it is available. The same can be said for musicians, who because of online venues including YouTube, Spotify, and iTunes, no longer have to rely on radio and music companies to distribute their songs.

Adding a new distribution channel might take the form of opening a retail location if you currently are a wholesaler, or it might be adding website sales in addition to your physical location. Or, to use an example from my career, when John Deere purchased United GreenMark, they bought a new distribution channel that enabled them to sell their existing products in United GreenMark outlets—a whole new layer of sales for them. Holy smokes, did that up their profitability!

Although they may not have originated the concept, the University of Phoenix was a huge contributor to turning the whole post-secondary education industry on its ear. The requirement of a brick-and-mortar college campus for a degree is evaporating as state universities jump into the game. How does this apply to distribution channels? At its core, doesn't a school distribute information and education? Talk about a distribution game changer, this revolutionary concept has exploded to all levels of education.

Origami Owl is a rags-to-riches story of a young lady with a dream that turned $350 into a multimillion-dollar powerhouse in the hypercompetitive custom jewelry industry. Beyond her creativity and hard work, what started out as a single shopping mall kiosk transformed itself entirely by adding a distribution channel reminiscent of companies such as Tupperware and Mary Kay, with independent sales associates, which Origami Owl calls independent designers. Through this model, the company primarily sells through home parties or independent designers' individual websites. Today, Origami Owl has more than 60,000 independent designers across the country, and every new associate who joins the company broadens the addressable market.

As I have said before, small to medium-sized businesses can reach for larger distribution channels too. Trucks and storefront rentals are available by the month, and internet sales and international import and distribution is getting more and more accessible. If your company doesn't currently own the resources necessary to achieve a broader distribution channel, you can lease them on a trial basis and test the concept at a lower level of risk. The payoff might be huge.

Because these networks have been extremely difficult and time consuming to erect, the ability to economically and efficiently move product from point A to point B is money to an investor. The companies that have focused on and perfected the distribution chain model can realize enormous valuation multipliers from investors.

From this point on in our discussion of the Rings, as we move closer and closer toward our target center, the air gets a bit thinner. The last three Rings are the most difficult to achieve, requiring a great deal of strategy, time, and effort. Although these Rings may seem daunting, the value they bring can be enormous.

Ring #3: Branding and Public Identification

Why does one clothing line logo give off a different-quality image than another? Why do we feel comfortable entering an H&R Block location when maybe we've never used a tax advisor before? Why do we feel the investment is worth it to buy a Mercedes-Benz when many, many less-expensive options exist?

In a word, branding.

People think they know what branding is, but a lot of the time it gets confused with marketing. Marketing is one piece of branding, but the branding concept is bigger than that—much bigger.

Branding is what you want the public to think and feel about your business. It's how a business tells its story to consumers.

Simon Sinek, the author of *Start with Why: How Great Leaders Inspire Everyone to Take Action*, says, "People don't buy what you do; they buy why you do it. And what you do simply proves what you believe." In his fantastic TED talk (titled "How Great Leaders Inspire Action"), Sinek explains that Dr. Martin Luther King Jr. wasn't a particularly gifted orator. Yet decades before the internet, 250,000 people showed up to the National Mall in Washington, D.C., to hear him speak because he had already been spreading the message about *what he believed.* People showed up because they also believed in his dream. **What you believe is what shows up in your brand.**

In a thousand different ways, businesses are explaining who they are and why you should be a part of their story. With its logo, with its commercials, with the paint color on the walls, a company communicates its values, its target demographic, and its aspirations through its brand story. That particular color of yellow that you only find on the golden arches? Branding. The soundtrack of jazz and folk that Starbucks plays and sells on CDs? (*Hello, additional revenue stream Ring #5.*) That sound is branding. The specific type of athletic yoga teacher that CorePower Yoga hires? That's branding too.

When building your own brand, all of these decisions deserve careful thought and research because they represent **your** image to the public. Your business personality is in your carefully crafted marketing language, your beautiful packaging, your products or services that hit the target demographics exactly where you want them to.

Wildly successful companies aren't winners just because of their quality products or services. They're successful because they are selling great stories to the right people.

And how do you figure out which people are the right ones? Research. Now don't panic. Research does not necessarily mean oodles of money and time. You can do market research on the internet or in your explorations of other similar companies. You can pull together an informal focus group to hear what consumers want and think. You can survey your base on your social media channels, or in person. Finding out if your marketing campaign worked can be answered with a two-question survey at the point of sale. Simply asking, "Have you ever shopped with us before?" and "How did you find out about us?" (or similar questions pertinent to your business) can help you ensure that your brand is reaching the people you intend it to. With the bevy of online tools available now, you do not have to be a big company to ensure that your target is the correct one. A basic SurveyMonkey survey sent to your email database is free.

So don't hold back. Fine-tune your brand by asking the questions that will attract your "right people." Questions like these:

1. Who is our target audience?
2. What do they really want?
3. How can we best meet their needs?
4. How much will they pay for our products or services?
5. How valuable are we to our customers?

What I'm getting at here is, do you know your customers and do they really know you? Ask the right questions and you'll know those answers. You will also know who is *not* going to participate in your story—which is great information to have because it means you can forgo wasting money trying to attract them. They aren't coming.

As you collect the valuable answers to those questions, blend them with your own spirit and mission. I learned about a smaller service company that discovered through its own inexpensive research (which included surveys, employee feedback from customer interactions, as well as website comments) that consumers wanted the company's associates to come out from behind their computers and be approachable humans. So the company built new welcoming processes that every employee now follows. It designed warm, approachable office spaces with branded color schemes. It made a series of video clips introducing the company's target market to the people who would be working on accounts—those clips also run on the website. These efforts encapsulated the ethos of the CEO, who sees great brand value in inclusion and open communication. Some of these themes may apply to your own brand.

Across the board, consumers appreciate human connection in their experiences—no matter the industry. So pull back the corporate curtain and show them the secret sauce —or at least parts of it— and you may just capture their loyalty too.

That said, investing in and committing to a broad branding campaign is not for everyone. That's partly why it is so valuable to an investor. It is also not the goal of every entrepreneur and business owner to be nationally or internationally known. That's okay. However, if your perception is that the size of your organization precludes you from this Ring, there are ways smaller companies can build a well-known local or regional presence too. Some align with others in the same industry and market themselves with national or international alliances. You see this often with service firms that are part of a worldwide group, thereby offering worldwide resources to their local clients. Another branding opportunity for smaller companies is to aggregate with other businesses in their area to market under a "shop local" banner. Downtown business associations and local organic or farm-to-table associations both use this regional marketing strategy.

Large or small, all businesses have the potential to leave their branding impressions in their targeted community.

Ring #2: Ability to Replicate and Scale

Replication—a procedure that can be duplicated—means the same thing in business as it does in science, not that you have to wear a lab coat. If your process yields the same results every time, even when various people perform it, then it's replicable. KFC chicken tastes the same whether it is cooked by a teenage fry cook or the Colonel himself. I think the key point in this definition is that the process must work even when you, the owner, aren't looking. To truly have replicable processes, they must be so well documented and ingrained that an entry-level employee can perform them to the well-established standards and performance expectations of the company.

For this Ring to have value, a potential investor must see your replicable processes functioning at very predictable and reliable metrics—*while at the same time concluding that duplicating your processes will be a steep and expensive hill to climb for your competitors.*

Once you have satisfied yourself that your methods can be replicated, ask yourself this very, very key question: "Can this process be scaled?" You are probably familiar with the phrase *economies of scale*, meaning the ability to add additional volume on the existing infrastructure, thereby adding profits (and value) faster than you are adding expenses. To an investor, Scalability = Economies of Scale. That is, for every dollar invested, profits and the value of the business increase quickly and at a higher amount than that invested dollar. This is an investor's dream situation and why this Ring is so valuable.

Computer software products are good examples of scalability, since the biggest costs are up front, in the creation, while mass production or opening up program access (like any production run) are done at progressively diminishing costs and increased profit per unit.

In fact, computer-based technology not only serves as an example of scaling, technology itself is the ideal tool to help other companies replicate and scale faster and more professionally than ever before. New technology tools not only improve business's ability to scale, they actually help owners document their systems and process workflows to better identify them as M advantages. If processes are documented and if the organization commits to them (even when no one is looking) then chances are they will improve the ability to scale!

Scalability happens in both product-based business as well as service-based. Yes, it may be easier to visualize expanding capacity in a business that produces cupcakes instead of personalized financial services or health care. However, examples of scaled finance and health companies are popping up around the country too. National names in accounting, insurance, and financial services continue to expand and scale with professionals who combine the repeatable "big city" processes of their firms with their own expertise to offer personalized services at local offices. While the individuals are not the same office to office, *the processes are.*

In health care, especially senior care, scalable franchises are rapidly claiming territory. Home Instead, a widely recognized name in home health care, appeared everywhere almost overnight. Assisted-living centers, rehab hospitals, and nursing homes are all spreading their geographic roots quickly to catch up with the demands of our aging population.

Here again, technology is driving opportunity in scalability, especially for service-based businesses that want to take their concepts to new heights. LegalZoom.com is a perfect example of this, but they're not the only one using technology's lower costs to share resources across multiple outlets. Hospital systems can leverage one top cardiologist who advises on several dozen cases every day, all over the country, through highly secure teleconferencing systems. Educators can speak to hundreds, perhaps thousands of students via online classes instead of just the thirty kids right in front of them.

For so long, it was thought that one-on-one service-based companies could not be scaled, but with evolving technology, it's simply no longer true. While scalability does require a commitment to keep up with technological enhancements in your industry and a vigorous dedication to documenting processes, being small is no longer an excuse for not trying to scale.

Word to the Wise: Whether product-based or service-based, a business built on or around an individual isn't scalable. For example, the kinds of businesses built on an owner's name or an individual's face ultimately set up artificial barriers to this Ring. If I had started a business called Tim's Taxes, it wouldn't have translated as well across multiple locations and states because customers would all want Tim the individual. Individuals just aren't replicable. So if you are thinking of starting a business or if you are evaluating this Ring in your new business model, consider the unintended limitations the business name might have on your expansion plans.

So now, in general, when considering whether you are ready to tackle this Ring, ask yourself these questions:

1. Are your processes standardized and predictable so that they could be reproduced by anyone—without you watching?

2. Are your procedures well documented?

3. Will a customer in one location have the exact same or similar experience as they would in any other location, city, or state?

If the answer to any of these questions is no, then your business is not the type for, or not yet ready for, this Ring.

In this Ability to Replicate and Scale Ring, an investor will be looking for the speed of this process. How fast can this replicable business model scale? The two attributes together equal an extraordinary compounding effect on value. Why? Because there is a certain predictability to the ROI for an investor. Just like in the Starbucks model. Because Starbucks has so much data on its location performances, replication and scaling extrapolates to predictable sales volumes, gross margins, operating costs, and pre-tax operating numbers. Bottom line, the combination of replication and scaling together extends exceptional enterprise value to a potential buyer, **but you have to be executing them both and be doing them really well to realize the full valuation impact of this Ring**.

I want to reinforce that there is an increased M value in each of the Rings, and the inability to replicate and scale does not mean you cannot score valuation drivers with other Rings.

Well, here we are, the bull's-eye of the target:

Ring #1: Power to Change Lives

This is the Lord of the Ring$. This level is in a category all its own, toward which the other six Rings build. By changing lives, I mean you have interrupted the standard way of doing business. You're in a whole new sphere that uses your core business as a means to a much more powerful end. Consider again the example of Tesla Motors, the premium electric car company. It is changing the way cars are made and in doing so, aiming at an environmentalist goal that is far beyond the way most car manufacturers think.

The more engaged you are in this Ring, the more positive effect you have on other Rings—especially your cultural environment. Thus, this Ring has an exponentially positive effect on your multiplier. If you can tap into a developing universe, the monetization is incalculable because you will have hit a growing movement right as it takes off.

To quote Simon Sinek again, he says people showed up for Martin Luther King Jr.'s "I Have a Dream" speech not because they wanted to see him, but because they wanted to be there for themselves. The public wants to support businesses that are conscious of the issues that are important to them. They are rooting for you to step up and make your decisions count. And, in return, they will spread the word far and wide about your brand, your products or services, and your investment in society.

Businesses are in a unique position to raise awareness about their Ring #1 issue. By using their platform to spread awareness, to donate company time and/or funds to a cause, by taking a position for the better good and marching toward it, companies can actually make profits and change people's lives simultaneously by building financial, social, and environmental capital. Making money can be a positive genesis for doing some real good in your community and around the world.

Consider these examples to get a better idea of Ring #1:
- Ben & Jerry's is an ice cream company that doesn't stop at fantastic ice cream. It uses its nationally recognizable brand to push for genetically modified organism (GMO) labeling and environmental sustainability. The company ensures that the cream and milk used in its wildly popular ice cream is from family farms and contains no hormones. Ben & Jerry's is leading by example, and its loyal customers recognize the integrity.
- New Belgium Brewing, the Fort Collins, Colorado–based beer brewery, is changing the way consumers and other brewers think about brewing. Since water is the number one ingredient in beer, it is in the brewery's interest to conserve as much water as it can in the beer-making process. Along the way, New Belgium funnels a portion of its profits to research and repair the Colorado River so it can continue to rely on this water source and help

preserve it for 30 million or so people who also depend on the river.

• Warby Parker, the eyeglass company, is interrupting a global monopoly that artificially elevates pricing, while donating to nonprofit partners. Instead of just donating glasses, their partners train men and women in developing countries to give basic eye exams and sell ultra-affordable glasses, which allows them to earn a real living as well. Warby Parker has found that this approach to donating builds less dependency and is more sustainable.

• United GreenMark, the irrigation pipe and sprinkler distribution company, developed an innovative drip system technology that conserved water usage by running only when the soil needed it, rather than by a set timer. Their systems were installed in municipalities and at universities, which saved thousands of gallons of water while at the same time earning profits for the company. These additional profits allowed the company to continually expand its technology, which in turn saved more and more of this precious resource.

• Patagonia is a designer of outdoor clothing and gear for the silent sports, including climbing, surfing, skiing and snowboarding, fly-fishing, and trail running. Its mission statement is to "Build the best product, cause no unnecessary harm, use business to inspire and implement solutions to the environmental crisis." To support this effort, Patagonia gives at least 1 percent of its sales to support environmental organizations around the world. In the company's own words: "As a company that uses resources and produces waste, we recognize our impact on the environment and feel a responsibility to give back. For us, it's not charity or traditional philanthropy. It's part of the cost of doing business. We call it our Earth Tax."

All of the above, along with the TOMS Shoes, mentioned in Chapter 1, are wonderful examples of companies that expand on their core mission to find ways to be a force for change in their industries as well as for the better good. More than just throwing money at a problem, they are dedicated to long-term policies that not only improve their communities but *also promote their own businesses by helping to continue their cause!*

While Ring #1 can be hard to wrap your head around, the good news is that it may already be at work in your company. All along, your business has been built around your unique core values. You started your business to address a problem. Likely you've been stymied by forces that impeded your progress along the way. Maybe you've even tried to do something about it. The businesses above are just the same. They looked at a problem from the macro level and then tried to implement a solution to get at the root of the problem. From producing efficient drip systems to high-quality ice cream with honest ingredients, these corporations were just trying to operate in a way that was *both* profitable *and* responsible. In this way, these people are changing the world by having provided a valuable service that their consumers use and feel good about supporting.

While perhaps not necessarily the goal, Ring #1 has the potential to be financially huge for you and your business by driving up your valuation M beyond compare. When companies are passionate about a cause that their community cares about, it's a game changer. When your sincere efforts to address a community concern of any size align with a wave of public sentiment, prepare yourself because **your multiple could be multiplying**!

Customers want to buy from businesses that they like. Although companies don't engage at this level solely for the financial advantages, the valuation reality is that the economics can be highly profitable. Want proof? Look at the profits from the companies listed above. Changing lives is a game changer, both for society *and* for your business.

***

In conclusion, investing time and money in any one or more of these Rings very likely separates you from your competition. In my experience, I have seen it to be well worth your time. Best of all, you don't have to run that business for years and years to recognize this added value. Often, if you can prove a Ring in concept, then that can translate to immediate value to a buyer. By further showing that it monetizes, well that is of even more exponential value to the organization. Of course, a proven track record with corroborating financial statements is generally needed to consummate a deal, but **in the speculative vector at which businesses are purchased today, a viable proven concept is already valuable.**

Chapter 4 Takeaways

1. The exponential impact on your company's valuation formula is driven by M; the Ring$ of Value are specifically targeted to increase M.

2. The extraordinary improvement in an enterprise's value resulting from the Rings is not limited by the size of your company.

3. Individual Ring attributes convey more than just financial value; they are your path to building a company that people believe in, want to work for, and feel good about patronizing.

CHAPTER 5

INCREASING VALUE THROUGH KNOWLEDGE

Some of the business broker industry secrets I have shared so far have been fairly technical. This next secret is deceptively simple and comes from my own "inside the deal room" experiences that I want to pass along to you now: Your knowledge can influence a buyer's purchase price and/or the speed of the transaction. **Simply put, your knowledge = buyer confidence.** If the buyer is confident, the deal goes more smoothly, quickly, and potentially, more PROFITABLY!

Seem too good to be true? Consider the following example. Imagine you are buying a car through a private party. As part of your due diligence, you ask the current owner, "Has this vehicle ever been in a wreck?" If the answer is a shrug of the shoulders or a "Well, that depends," that is a big red flag. It should make your eyebrows narrow, because it means the owner either doesn't know or is hiding something. Neither is good for you as the buyer. In that situation, you would run from the deal as fast as your feet would take you.

As a business owner, when you engage in these types of conversations with your potential business investors, you want to keep their perspective in mind; what is important (or valuable) to them? As they work through their due diligence process, you want them feeling confident that you have disclosed any and all pertinent data and ensured a high level of trust. Every single interaction with a possible buyer is a test of those factors.

Such conversations can either open the door a bit wider or slam it closed. The entire purpose of this book is to get you to that conversation and impart a mastery of the business fundamentals that will enhance your business's valuation in a transaction.

The next set of skills we're going to focus on is outside the Ring$ of Value. I listed the day-to-day financial minutia as business noise because your time spent in these areas imparts no direct additional transactional value. But here's the paradox: You still have to know what's going on in your financial world, and you have to know it exceedingly well. To continue our metaphor, the impetus is on you, the driver of the vehicle, to be aware of the regularly required maintenance and the needs of the vehicle in order to keep it operating at maximum efficiency. Whether you change the oil (prepare the statements) yourself or you hire professional help isn't the point. You can delegate, but never ever delegate the working knowledge of those levers that drive your business and its value. If you have ever said, "I let my so-and-so handle all of that" and either don't understand the process yourself and/or never inspect the results, you're guilty of this deficiency.

Without financial literacy, you're driving blind. If potential investors suspect that you lack command of your own business's vital metrics, they may question the entire transaction. If they begin to question the transaction, they may end up offering you less or, worse yet, walk away completely. While being financially fluent may not get you a deal, the lack of it can certainly kill the deal.

I have come to think of knowledge as one of the most underutilized factors in a business sale. I have seen it make and break deals. This is because quick, honest, and accurate responses to investor queries lead to an increase in trust. And when trust is high, the speed of the transaction increases. As Stephen R. Covey explains in his book *The Speed of Trust*, when trust is high, speed goes up and costs go down. Gaining trust requires a combination of character traits *and proven competency.* Covey says your capabilities and your results are two crucial factors in earning trust. Conversely, without trust, a transaction slows, the smallest of points begin to get questioned and become distractions to the buyer. When this happens, the chance of a transaction at all is much less likely. Certainly, the potential reward that the Ring$ of Value can garner is lost.

Admittedly, quantifying the numerical value of your knowledge's effect on a transaction can be squishy. You're much more likely to feel the pain of its absence than to note its presence. The difference is a negotiation that loses steam and peters out versus the big smiles and handshakes all around after a satisfactory closure. While I can't put a number on it, I have witnessed that **knowledge does build trust. And trust begets speed. Speed is your friend in a sale.**

From My Experience
The Wild Ride

Let's go back to the story from Chapter 2 about United GreenMark, the irrigation distribution company that had been purchased by that private equity group. While I referred to the experience as a wild ride, this was in large part due to their insatiable appetite for data and numbers. They devoured our numbers faster than I, as CFO, had ever developed them in the past and constantly came back for more and more and more. However, this forced learning process taught me how to gather large amounts of information and distill it down in a way that others would understand it and so I could respond on my feet to rapid-fire boardroom questioning. With piercing questions from the left, right, and then left again, my responses needed to be verbalized in a way that would connect with and satisfy each person at the table who authored a question.

I will never forget this one quarterly board meeting in particular when one weak response took all the momentum out of the room. To this day I am still so thankful that they did not direct this particular question to me. The irrigation distribution company president was attempting to explain the reason for a year-over-year drop in revenues. He said it was caused by the current year's unusually strong storm season, which had resulted in widespread regional flooding. It seemed like a logical enough position to me, yet once the president had finished the overview, the room got almost completely quiet. The private equity group chairman was apparently not buying the analysis that there would be less demand for irrigation products when people's yards were sliding down the street. In a snarky tone that I will never forget, he asked, "Well didn't it rain last year too?" With that one sassy question, it seemed like our entire presentation had suddenly crashed to a dead stop.

There really wasn't anything the company president could have done or said differently in that instance. Sometimes revenues rise and fall despite everyone's best efforts. If the flow of a conversation or transaction is interrupted, everything you have worked toward can get derailed. Conversely, successful question sessions can energize both parties, shuttling a deal down the fast track, which usually means more money too. That happened with this same company a few months later.

Because we were owned by this group, we were always on the market for sale. To the United GreenMark internal employee base, all went quiet for a time on the transactional front. Then, seemingly out of nowhere, John Deere Landscapes started investigating the possibility of purchasing us to complete the West Coast hole in its nationwide irrigation distribution network. This was clearly a move by John Deere into Ring #4, Distribution Channels. Also, this acquisition allowed the company to nationally brand its new John Deere Landscapes division, which it was using to improve its Branding and Public Identification, Ring #3. This new division was also a new Revenue Stream, Ring #5, in that John Deere was expanding beyond its core green equipment product lines into irrigation product lines (underground PVC pipes, sprinkler heads, and timers, etc.). Relying on the strength of all of our financial information, the whole transaction was done within just about three months. From out of nowhere to closing in three months—are you kidding me?

John Deere's decision makers made it a point to include me in the negotiations. They said the integrity of the data I provided allowed them to relax some of their normal protocols and thus expeditiously close the deal. That knowledge/trust/speed thing was beneficial for both sides of the transaction: From the buyer's perspective it lowered the professional fees associated with the transaction and allowed the company to start selling product sooner. The seller certainly benefited by getting the highest value for its business and by actually getting the cash in the bank! A true win-win scenario.

That's when I learned for myself how something as seemingly intangible as knowledge can have such a tangible impact on a business's value and/or on closing a deal at all.

Financial Literacy

Hopefully that story convinces you to honestly assess your financial literacy. You may think you know your financials inside and out, but remember that the types of questions you'll get from a would-be investor are very different from the questions you will field from your own internal team. They can be uncomfortable conversations, or they may not be uncomfortable at all; it's your choice. Which would you prefer? Well, I am here to help you tip the balance of the teeter-totter conversation in your favor!

Those who possess financial savvy quickly earn the trust of potential buyers, interested investors, or current stakeholders and can expect to move on expeditiously through negotiations with a sense of confidence.

Two Types of Acquisition

If your company may one day be for sale, you need to know what types of transactions you could encounter. The two acquisition types I want you to be aware of are an asset purchase and a capital stock purchase.

In general terms, an asset purchase is when buyers pick out only the components of a company they are interested in buying and acquire them. It might be all of the company's assets or just the receivables or inventory, certain store locations, the brand name of a particular product line or service technology, patents or trademarks, revenue streams, or some combination thereof. Once these components are purchased, they are then placed in a new or existing entity.

An asset purchase isn't necessarily bad for the seller, but as a seller you just need to be aware of what it means. Again, don't think like the seller, think like the buyer. If given the choice, buyers will only buy the components of value to them. Sounds obvious, but on the flip side, you as the seller will be left with assets of little or no remaining value and generally all of the debt. So from the sale proceeds, you then must retire any outstanding obligations.

The alternative to an asset purchase is a capital stock purchase. Here, actual stock shares of the existing company are purchased, giving that investor an immediate pro rata ownership in the entire enterprise. The purchase can be for a minority ownership position, a majority investment, or a full 100 percent outright purchase.

The concern for investors when they choose this type of purchase is that it incorporates both the assets *and the liabilities* of the company. Liabilities will include those that are known, unknown, and contingent. So as a seller, you can naturally expect even more concentration during the due diligence process from a buyer investigating your liabilities before closing a transaction.

On the other hand, a very key added benefit to buyers in a stock purchase is that they have acquired all the employees, the vendor relations and terms, the goodwill of the existing company, etc., etc. In other words, the company just continues on under new ownership.

In my experience, asset purchases are becoming more common than stock purchases. The more sophisticated buyers generally already have an entity readied to receive these new positive assets without any residual concerns over the prior liabilities of the seller.

The moral of this story? Any transaction has a certain velocity to it. You don't want to be the speed bump that slows or derails the talks. So, you as a seller need to be aware of what types of deal structures may come your way. It is my role to get you as prepared as possible to negotiate your best deal with either type of sale transaction.

Chapter 5 Takeaways

1. Knowledge in a transaction can equal more MONEY to you.

2. Never forget that knowledge builds trust. And trust begets speed. Speed is your friend in any sale.

3. Be prepared for any transaction structure by knowing the two types: asset purchase or capital stock purchase.

CHAPTER 6

TOOLS FOR SUCCESS: THE COMPONENTS OF FINANCIAL STATEMENTS

Continuing with the theme of financial literacy, you need to know some accounting basics. Again, you can hire professionals to help you through your regular accounting and a business sale, but you must also have at least a base level of knowledge yourself. If this is new information, pour yourself a cup of coffee and dig in; these few sections are important. It's fascinating, and I love it, but I know some people lose interest fast. Stick with me; I will go quickly. If you know this stuff, read it anyway. Education, as one esteemed philosopher once put it, is never wasted.

I promise I will only talk about three key statements contained within a financial report package: the balance sheet, statement of income, and the statement of cash flows. Since I told myself that I do not want this to be an accounting textbook, I will commit to only covering the very basic formats that you will likely see again and again in your business.

Balance Sheets

A balance sheet is a detailed list of the assets, liabilities, and owner's equity of a business entity as of a specific date, usually at the close of the last day of a month, quarter, or year. Although the information contained in a balance sheet gives you a snapshot of your business, it's important to keep in mind that the snapshot is only for that moment in time. By the next day, the information on these very important statements is already starting to be old news. Back in my public accounting days, I remember packaging beautifully bound end-of-year statements for the clients, knowing that by the time they were released to them a few months after the period covered, they were already old news to the users. Don't misunderstand what I am saying; these statements are useful tools because they allow quick assessment of the financial condition of a company *at that moment*, but the farther away from that exact statement date, the less relevant they can be. For example, cash in the bank at the end of business on a December 31st balance sheet might not mean very much to a reader if he or she is reviewing the statement in the middle of the summer.

While date sensitive, balance sheets do literally show the balance of a company's assets, liabilities, and owner or shareholder equity. The only formula I need you to know here is **Assets = Liabilities + Shareholder Equity**, which is the basic formation of the balance sheet. The sum of the company's assets equals what you owe against the assets plus any cumulative shareholder or owner equity that you have in the business.

Assets are listed in the order of their expected conversion to cash. So cash is first, followed by receivables, inventory, if applicable, and so on. These current assets are then anything expected to be converted to cash within the next twelve months. Below these items, we find the more permanent, or fixed assets, such as equipment, buildings, and land. From those we subtract depreciation to get the net book value of your fixed assets.

On the other side of the balance sheet are liabilities, and like assets, they are generally listed chronologically as the debts become due and subtotaled as either current or long-term. Equity is then shown beneath liabilities and is made up of your capital stock balances and any cumulated earnings—called retained earnings (or the company earnings still retained in the business).

Shown below is the balance sheet of a hypothetical company I have called Mountaintop Ski & Sports. The balance sheet is meant to help you visualize just how clean and simple all of these words and definitions from above can actually be.

Let's take a look:

MOUNTAINTOP SKI & SPORTS
Balance Sheet
Year End

ASSETS

CURRENT ASSETS:			
Cash	$ 125,000		
Inventory	500,000		
Other Current Assets	75,000		
Total Current Assets		$	700,000
FIXED ASSETS:			
Property and Equipment	400,000		
Less: Accumulated Depreciation	(100,000)		
Total Net Fixed Assets			300,000
TOTAL ASSETS		$	1,000,000

LIABILITIES AND EQUITY

CURRENT LIABILITIES:			
Accounts Payable	$ 250,000		
Line of Credit	100,000		
Total Current Liabilities		$	350,000
LONG-TERM LIABILITIES			
Note Payable			250,000
TOTAL LIABILITIES			600,000
EQUITY:			
Capital Stock	25,000		
Retained Earnings	375,000		
Total Equity			400,000
TOTAL LIABILITIES & EQUITY		$	1,000,000

While there are a lot of key numbers and metrics that come off the balance sheet, I am only going to ask you to learn two: the current ratio and of course your E. The current ratio is your company's liquidity ratio, which measures your ability to pay your obligations. The formula to calculate this ratio is **Current Assets / Current Liabilities**. The higher the ratio, the more capable the company is of paying its bills. On the contrary, a ratio under one indicates that current liabilities are greater than current assets, which would suggest the inability to satisfy debts as they come due. In our example, the current ratio is $700,000 / $350,000 for a two. Lenders like high (two or more) current ratios.

As we have learned, E is your equity. Not only is equity a very important indicator of the stability of a business, it can also be very, very valuable in a transaction! A company's equity is the difference between all of its assets and all of its liabilities, or $1,000,000 - $600,000 = $400,000, as shown by the subtotals above. Therefore, whatever price someone would pay for the business operations (P x M), just tack on another $400,000 for their E!

Statements of Income

Our second statement is one that many business owners use with regularity to check on revenues, operating costs, and of course their bottom line.

A statement of income, sometimes called an income statement or a profit and loss statement, is a summary of the revenue and the expenses of a business entity for a specific period of time—for example a month or a year. They are typically formatted like this: **Total Revenues - Costs and/or Expenses = Net Income.**

Below is an example of a standard statement of income to better visualize this layout:

MOUNTAINTOP SKI & SPORTS
Statement of Income
Twelve Months

OPERATING REVENUES:		
Merchandise Sales	$ 4,500,000	
Boot & Ski Rentals	500,000	
Total Operating Revenues		$ 5,000,000
COST OF GOODS SOLD		2,750,000
GROSS PROFIT		2,250,000
OPERATING EXPENSES:		
Salary Expenses	1,750,000	
Rent Expense	125,000	
Insurance Expenses	100,000	
Advertising & Promotion	50,000	
Telephone & Utilities	15,000	
Office Expenses	10,000	
Total Operating Expenses		2,050,000
OPERATING INCOME/"EBITDA"		200,000
NON-OPERATING EXPENSES:		
Depreciation Expense	15,000	
Interest Expense	10,000	
Total Non-operating Expenses		25,000
INCOME BEFORE INCOME TAXES		175,000
INCOME TAX EXPENSE		75,000
NET INCOME/NET PROFIT		$ 100,000

Operating revenues is the first category of figures represented on an income statement. That is all the money the company earned in operating the business in that period of time, a figure also referred to as gross revenues, gross sales, or total operating revenues.

For a product-based company, immediately below revenues are the costs associated with those revenue-generating items that were sold, titled the costs of goods sold. The subtotal derived after deducting the costs of goods sold from the revenues is called gross profit or gross margin, a key number indeed.

From this gross profit subtotal, or directly from total revenues if you are a service-based company, we deduct operating expenses: salaries, advertising, rent, utilities, and so on. These selling/overhead/administrative–type costs are shown below the costs of goods sold because they aren't directly linked to Mountaintop Ski & Sports' expenses of getting skis and boards into customers' hands. The presentation philosophy of an income statement is simply an attempt to match the costs and expenses against the revenues that those expenditures helped generate in that period. Unlike costs of goods sold, these general types of expenses tend not to vary directly with sales. Depending on your revenue sources, subtracting these operating expenses from either the operating revenues or gross profit, you arrive at operating income if the number is positive or operating deficit if this is a negative number.

This subtotal is the profit or loss that results from standard business operations before interest, income taxes, depreciation, and amortization are deducted. Yes, this is the all-important **EBITDA** figure that we talked about earlier.

Operating income/EBITDA is also the subtotal calculated before any unusual items or expenses, so an investor or potential buyer can quickly compare year-over-year revenues, gross profit, and operating income of a company to arrive at a pretty accurate picture of a company's financial direction and earning potential.

What I find really interesting here (and as a matter of fact, it applies directly to the business valuation process we are talking about) is the theory for placing any income and expense items below this operating income/EBITDA subtotal. Not only aren't these items directly associated with generating the operating income figures above, but more important, how each company chooses to finance itself, depreciate its assets, or even determine its income tax bracket is unique and individual to that company. As I have discussed before, these individual items are not necessarily what another entity might have as their circumstance. Therefore, these non-operating expenses are itemized at the bottom of the statement.

If you step back and think about what this standard presentation does, you'd see that it tends to put all companies on an equal evaluation basis by just comparing pure operating revenues versus pure operating costs—or more to the point, comparing one company's EBITDA to another's. Any and all other extraordinary-type gains or losses, financing, or income taxes are dealt with separately and below this operating revenue/EBITDA subtotal.

Continuing on, after deducting the company's income taxes as the last expense item shown on an income statement, the final bottom-line amount is titled net income if positive or net loss if negative.

Much can be gleaned from a company's income statement. For example, many financial professionals interpret and extrapolate from current or past income statement performances to find an indication of things to come. By looking at sales revenue trends, margins, overhead run rates, personnel costs, and comparing all these metrics to industry standards, a very accurate picture of the health and vitality of a company is revealed. As an owner, you can perform these same side-by-side market comparisons by looking at your own industry data and any competitors' information you might have to see where you are performing better and where there is room to improve. Plus, with your growing knowledge about valuations, I am sure that your own company's P will take on a whole new measure of importance.

So, you rising valuation pro, what is Mountaintop's EBITDA? That's right, $200,000.

Word to the Wise

Throughout my experiences, I occasionally come across she-nanigans buried in income statements. Maybe someone is paying a higher than market-rate salary to a spouse, or maybe the cost of goods sold is fudged a bit. These inconsistencies stick out like a sore thumb to someone like me who can quickly pierce through such attempts by applying experience and analytics. Expense ratios like that are outside the normal range of revenue to expenditures for the industry. **And, if I can see these shenanigans, know that savvy financial buyers or investors can see them as well.** When this happens in transactions, it deflates the buyer's opinion of the company—that whole trust thing I discussed earlier. Rest assured, such findings by potential buyers or savvy investors will have just that deflating impact; the result will either be a reduction of your valuation or worse, they will just walk away because of an integrity issue.

We all know people in business who think they are getting away with this sort of trickery, usually justifying it as an effort to keep their tax burden low. However, these strategies will invariably come back to haunt them because *true tax deductions are one thing; tax avoidance is another.* Owners need to be straightforward about their company revenues and expenses, even if that means paying the appropriate amount of income taxes. From the perspective of a buyer or investor, monkey business in the company's books leads to a loss of trust and credibility, which can kill a deal.

Statements of Cash Flows

A statement of cash flows is probably my favorite tool for evaluating businesses because they allow a reader to see where cash has been generated from and how it is being spent. Ironically, they are the least used but the *most useful* of all the business tools we'll discuss. Also called a statement of changes, this tool shows the link between a balance sheet and an income statement. It shows what you really did with your money. When applied in conjunction with the other financial statements, the statement of cash flows can also be employed as a means to analyze past and future profitability of a company.

A statement of cash flows classifies cash receipts and cash payments by three types of activities: operating activities, investing activities, and financing activities. By separating sources this way, it is easy to identify how and where a company has been successful when juxtaposing multiple years. For example, this statement shows whether you're borrowing money to finance your business or whether the business is solvent enough to support itself. It can also reveal if you extended too much credit to your customers or when lines of credit are getting used, thus leveraging a company, sometimes overly so. If your accounts receivable or line of credit jumps from $500,000 to $1,000,000, the company in question may be going backward in its management of cash, unless there are other justifying reasons for these signals.

Let's take a look at a sample statement of cash flows for Mountaintop:

MOUNTAINTOP SKI & SPORTS
Statement of Cash Flows
Twelve Months

CASH FLOWS FROM OPERATING ACTIVITIES			
Net Income			$ 100,000
Adjustments to cash provided by operating activities:			
Depreciation on property and equipment			15,000
Changes in:			
Inventory	$	(75,000)	
Other current assets		10,000	
Accounts payable		(25,000)	
Total changes			(90,000)
Net cash from operating activities			25,000
CASH FLOWS FROM INVESTING ACTIVITIES			
Cash advanced on line of credit			50,000
CASH FLOWS FROM FINANCING ACTIVITIES			
Payments on note payable			(25,000)
NET INCREASE IN CASH			50,000
CASH, beginning of year			75,000
CASH, end of year			$ 125,000

The first section, cash flows from operating activities, reflects how much money was made as a result of products sold or services rendered. Changes to accounts receivable, inventory, or accounts payable are reflected in this portion of the cash flows statement. I always look at accounts receivable compared to inventory because profitable companies quickly convert inventory to receivables, and ultimately to cash. If there is too much invested in inventory, that's a signal that portends future loss because stale inventory is rarely sold at full price. That's as true for a bakery's stale bread as it is for a ski shop with too much invested in last year's styles. Counterintuitively, when accounts payable increase over time it shows good cash management, since vendor terms are being utilized. That's a thumbs-up from investors' point of view because they can then also see this cash being reinvested back into the business.

Below operating activities you note a line entry that reads cash flows from investing activities. This section includes cash going out to cover the costs of asset investments and cash coming in from credit lines or profits from investment activities.

The final section is cash flows from financing activities. This area reflects long-term loans and changes in debt. It is also indirectly an indicator of the company's cash management ability, in that long-term financing actions can impact today's cash flow. For example, perhaps an owner wants to pay off the mortgage on his land early. If he or she did that, it would be seen here and a buyer may wonder why a company would use its precious cash to pay off a long-term debt early. This may actually be deemed a demerit in a potential investor's eyes. Early payment of a long-term asset doesn't add any real value to the business, and that cash may have been better utilized for current debt responsibilities rather than pre-paying debt. Poor cash management and poor judgment may lead to NO transaction.

While the statement of cash flows is used less often in your day-to-day operations, it is a vital if you run your business every day like it's for sale, because it can show you how an investor will actually be assessing the movement of your company's assets. Making a statement of cash flows part of your vernacular increases your financial literacy and brings you up to the level at which your investors operate. Any educated buyer who possesses the wherewithal to pay serious money for your business is going to ask for this statement. Be prepared, and have it ready.

Beyond the above details, what are your "have to knows" about statements of cash flows? First and foremost, note that the bottom two lines in our sample statement, the cash Mountaintop started the year with and the cash it ended the year with, increased by $50,000. Second, note how much of that $50,000 increase from above is from net cash from operating activities. If your answer is $25,000 of the $50,000, you are right! From this point, you can now continue to dig deeper into the numbers on this statement to be ahead of what any buyer might quiz you on when you have to explain your own.

The Bottom Line

Now that you have waded through the nitty-gritty numbers, let me boil down the main lesson. The noise that draws you away from building lasting value can be a distraction, or it can be an asset. Savvy business owners know how these financial tools work. They may choose to delegate their preparation, but at the same time they understand them so well that they are *using them* to help guide the operation. By showing a firm grasp on the balance sheets, income statements, and the statements of cash flows, owners build trust and standing in a deal. Trust leads to speed. And speed equals money to you, the seller—remember?

When John Deere came knocking on the door of United GreenMark, the credibility built by knowing the numbers inside and out set the stage for a quick, lucrative transaction. The buyers weren't buying the company because of the financial information, but it sure helped immensely that the statements were accurate, up-to-date, and attractively packaged. Every time they kicked the tires, they got the right response. That high level of trust helped establish the eventual valuation of United GreenMark.

Once that relationship was solid, John Deere grabbed on tight and said, "We'll take it!"

Chapter 6 Takeaways

1. You can delegate the preparation of financial statements, but owners must really, really understand them and know how to use them for the company's benefit.

2. The primary reports contained within a financial statement package are the balance sheets, income statements, and the statements of cash flows.

3. Learn to read and see your financial statements as an investor would; it will increase your knowledge and credibility, your company's metric performances, and ultimately its salability.

CHAPTER 7

HOW WELL DO YOU REALLY KNOW YOUR BUSINESS?

If you run your business every day like it's for sale, there is really only one requirement you need to nail every day, and it is also something a potential investor wants to know: **Are you performing better than your competition or anyone in your space?** But let's take it one step further. As a business owner, I don't want you to just compare yourself solely to your competition. That suggests that you are only playing to the level of your field. The overall theme of the Ring$ of Value is that you are doing things that your competition cannot even imagine doing. So are you?

In addition to this daily challenge, you also want to ask these questions: Is the company improving its performance? Are our business metrics improving this month, this quarter, this year? Are we following the industry or, with the guidance of the Rings, are we expanding our vision and opportunities? Beyond that, are we really heading toward our mission statement? And even more than that, are we making a difference?

The simplicity of these questions belies the complexity of finding answers, because answering yes doesn't necessarily translate to earning more profit year after year. Referencing the seven Ring$ of Value, I have talked about building a strong cultural environment, the power of innovation, creating new revenue streams, creating new distribution channels, positive branding and public identification, increasing the ability to replicate and scale, and the power of changing lives—all value-added propositions that not only affect profit but also the multiplier in our $V = P \times M + E$ formula.

As I have previously discussed, being overly concerned with daily sales and cash flows, vendor issues, and personnel decisions are all facets of business life that, while immensely important, can potentially pull your attention away from investing in the Ring$ of Value. They do not get you off the hook. At the Ring$ of Value level, you have to be better than that.

The Matrix of Your Metrics

As said earlier, there are certain things that *cannot* be delegated in your business without constant inspection and oversight. Keep your eyes not only on all the balls you have in the air but on the details and processes of each as well.

No matter which of the Ring$ of Value you are giving your attention to at any one time, data-driven results require facts and figures that provide insight into the effectiveness of your operations. Financial statements most assuredly provide an entrepreneur with a scorecard for how well the business model is working. Being cognizant of the components that make up these financial statements allows owners to form goals and continually make course corrections as problems arise.

For example, are you growing at a faster rate than your competitors? Are you creating value that is outpacing industry standards? Achieving answers to these questions requires the goals themselves, but just as important, it requires the tools to track and monitor your performance relative to these goals. The onus is on you to plan, evaluate, and adjust, in essence to have a continually updated business vision. Many people assume (incorrectly) that a business plan is only required in getting a business up and running. Not so. One of your future investor's first information requests will most assuredly be for a copy of your current business plan. Not having one is a sign of inefficiency—like a car without a steering wheel. After all, how can you arrive at a destination that doesn't exist? Think of your mission statement and vision statement as your map. Think of your ongoing business plan as your step-by-step directions for how to get there. Think of your succession plan as a motivator to run your business every day like it's for sale. Oh, and most important, make certain that all three of these include engagement in the Rings of Value.

Judge for Yourself

In the next sections of this chapter, we'll start with a few light questions designed to identify the depth of your knowledge of your business as of right now. These questions have many purposes:

1. They will serve as a guide for how effectively you are able to run your business every day like it's for sale.

2. Your score will show your readiness for dealing with any potential buyer or investor.

3. And finally, the questions will show if you and your company have reached a level where you can invest a certain amount of your efforts in the Rings of Value.

I strongly recommend that you come back to these questions as a part of your annual review process and use them as one of your tools to mark your own increased literacy.

Internal Metrics Quiz

(Circle one answer per question.)

Balance Sheet

1. What level of CPA-prepared financial statement do you have?

No CPA statements   Compiled   Reviewed/Audited

2. How do your assets compare to your liabilities?

Don't know   L > A   A > L

3. Which direction is your current ratio trending?

Not sure   Decreasing   Increasing

4. Over the last three years, your retained earnings are going:

Not sure   Down   Up

5. How many stockholders in your company?

1   Fewer than 5   Greater than 5

Income Statement

1. Over the past three years, year-over-year revenues are:

Not sure   Decreasing   Increasing

2. Over the past three years, your gross profit % on your products and/or services is:

Not sure   Decreasing   Increasing

3. Over the last three years, salaries as a % of revenues are trending:

Not sure   Up   Down

4. Over the last three years, as % of revenues, your overall operating expenses are:

Not sure   Increasing   Decreasing

5. Over the past three years, your EBITDA is:

Not sure   Decreasing   Increasing

For the ten questions above, give yourself a score value of -1 for every answer you circled in the first column, any answer in the middle column give yourself a 0, and for an answer in the far right column give yourself a score value of 1. Scores of 7 or more mean that you are on the right track; below that, you have some work to do.

What Data Are You Tracking?

This is a hard question to answer in general terms because the meaningful metrics vary from industry to industry. There are some basic data points that you're probably already using: year-over-year sales, sales compared to your business plan, operating income and expense ratios such as revenues/employee, or perhaps even EBITDA.

I often encourage companies to give at least as much attention to their statements of cash flows as they do their income statements or balance sheets. One, it is a great way to judge the ongoing progress of your operation. And two, potential buyers and interested investors will always take a hard look at the company's cash flow as a means of understanding your sources and uses of funds, and ultimately the company's valuation.

My suggestion is to identify the performance metrics that will catch the eye of would-be buyers or investors; those are the ones that will benefit the company the most. The juicy details of your financial statements aren't always apparent to new users, but given your transformation through this book, you are ready to really set some value-enhancing goals for your company and to develop the tools to effectively track its progress.

Once you have identified your current internal indicators, compare years side by side. Look at how those current numbers relate to the same time period for the previous year or years. What do the metrics tell you about the evolution of your product or service lines, your customer mix, and your standing in your particular industry? Are you trending up or down? How would a potential investor view your progress?

Remember my United GreenMark story about the rain? When the investor asked, "Didn't it rain last year?" he wasn't being facetious; he was asking for an explanation about the differences in year-to-year revenues. He really just wanted to know why performance during the current year was down versus the plan and the prior year.

Look at your profits compared to your budget *and* your industry. Most businesspeople just look at the trailing twelve-month results (aka, the previous year), which are constructive and useful, but in some ways that's like driving a car using only the rear- and side-view mirrors. My most effective coaching tool is to do a future cash flow model, knowing that to fuel your forward motion you need to look through the windshield at what's ahead of you. Where are you going and more important, do you have the "four Ps" (people, products/services, processes, and plan) in place to get you there?

As a business owner you want tools that tell you how well you're doing, but you also want tools that help you see more accurately and more quickly if you've gotten off track. When we start our businesses, we create a vision for the short-, mid-, and long-term. We also create a marketing strategy for the products or services the business is built upon. It's ironic how often we forget to track or reevaluate and update our progress, isn't it?

Digging a little deeper, some businesses track profitability per transaction. If the industry standard is, say, $225 in gross profit per transaction, and you're only at $200 per transaction, one of your goals will be to surpass that standard. However, if you're operating as if you're selling the business, then you will want to be aiming for $250 or above in profit per transaction. The accomplishment of such a goal obviously improves your P, but perhaps more important, it lifts you above the industry standard, which adds to your multiplier in our $V = P \times M + E$ formula— another win-win.

I can almost hear you saying, "Easier said than done." Yes, it is easier said than done if all of your energy is focused on just the daily business noise issues. That is where engagement in the Ring$ of Value becomes so vital. As a Rings business owner, you should be devoting one day a week or perhaps even more to being a visionary. Find ways to explore concepts that will catapult your business to the performance metrics you only dreamed about before. That is how true value is built. Moreover, you'll have the special attention of investors your competition will never have.

Internal and external metrics go hand in hand. One shows your current standing, the other illuminates where you need to be. How are you going to drive your metrics going forward? The Rings answer is that you're going to drive them first **by knowing how others in your industry are performing at certain levels and acting accordingly**. And second, you are going to drive them **by identifying which best practices and standards are facilitating your Rings' performances**. If you're not performing on at least the same level as your industry's leaders, buyers aren't going to pay you more for your company. In fact, they're probably going to pay you less, if they pay you anything at all.

External Metrics Quiz

(Circle one answer per question.)

The Competition

1. Do you know your competitors' unique selling proposition?

What is that?　　No　　Yes

2. What amount of the market do you have versus your competition?

Not sure　　They have a larger share　　We have a larger share

3. Do you know your competitors' key operating ratios?

Not sure　　No　　Yes

4. Do you know why some buy from your competitor versus your company?

Not sure　　No　　Yes

5. Does your competition have employees whom you would rather have work for your company?

Not sure　　Yes　　No

Industry

1. Do you attend industry association meetings?

No　　Rarely　　Frequently

2. Do you regularly disseminate industry information throughout your company?

It's not available　　No　　Yes

3. How do your company's key operating ratios compare to your industry?

Not sure　　Not as good　　Better

4. As a whole, is your industry:

       Constricting   Not sure   Expanding

5. Does your company have new innovative products/services on the horizon?

         No   Not sure   Yes

For the ten questions above, give yourself a score value of -1 for every answer you circled in the first column, any answer in the middle column give yourself a 0, and for an answer in the far right column give yourself a score value of 1. Scores of 7 or more mean that you are on the right track; below that, you have some work to do.

Where Can You Find External Data?

The importance of participating in your industry's community cannot be overstated. These people are your competitors, yes, but they are also invaluable sources of information. For example, many industries have national associations. As members, companies input financial information that is then consolidated and shared back to all the contributing members. This is critical insider information compiled without specific company names associated with it. These figures tell the participants where the profession is headed and how their firm stacks up against the opposition.

Similarly, construction companies, for example, can submit their operating results to builder exchanges and surveys, which in turn disseminate the information nationally and regionally to members. Chances are there are professional membership groups available for you too. Attend the meetings and listen during those boring lunches. The data you seek may be hiding there.

How does this relate to the Ring$ of Value? Look at Ring #4, Distribution Channels. The more you know about your industry, the better you can plan your network expansion, and believe me, interested buyers and potential investors will take notice. Look at

Ring #3, Branding and Public Identification. The better acquainted you are with your industry and its members, the more opportunities you will see for creating a brand uniquely your own. Many business professionals don't utilize the value of the information available to them. Use others' pontificating and carelessness to your advantage.

Within the category of external data, there are crucial gauges that might seem out of the box to some. Many owners forget to factor in environmental, social, and economic trends that impact their industries. For example, a huge factor in the success or failure of our fictitious Mountaintop Ski & Sports is weather. Not paying attention to the *Farmers' Almanac* and meteorological forecasts for the coming year might result in huge inventory overstock errors or, conversely, a dearth of stock. The last thing a retailer wants to do is build up a bunch of unsold inventory or come up short when the spring skiers begin to show up. Knowing the date of the first and last snow sounds simple, but our sports shop owners will need to track this information religiously; a windfall of snow will positively impact their sales in exactly the same way as a scarcity of snow will impact it in negative terms. You have to expand and contract your business with the ebb and flow of information and lifestyle changes.

This type of tracking impacts every industry, not just retail. To give a service-based example, think about the veterinarian practice I referenced in Chapter 2. It is probably a safe bet that not too many veterinarians read *Us Weekly* or *People* magazine for professional research, but when you consider how many people buys dogs based on the number of famous people who have a particular breed, maybe they should. Knowing that the current celebrity du jour owns a Maltese, shih tzu, or pug might lead savvy veterinarians to seek specialized training in the needs of small dogs, thereby helping differentiate their practice and better establish a public identification by branding and marketing themselves as experts or specializing in these species. That's how your put the Ring$ of Value into action!

Your Market

Beyond your internal and external financial metrics, knowing why your products or services sell requires an understanding of your market. Why do your clients come to you, and how invested are they? It is said that customers are loyal to you as long as your prices are lower than your competitors'. Is that true for you?

You probably already know who your top customers are, but how much is your business actually profiting from these relationships? Breaking down profit numbers generated by your top accounts helps you see how beneficial the time spent with these relationships really is. Using that magnifying lens to get deep into your profits is the difference between being successful and knowing *why* you are successful. When you can explain to potential investors or interest buyers *why* you are successful, expect them to listen.

Dollars surely tell most of the story, but not all of it. After exploring and understanding the hard numbers, I recommend tracking the soft metrics that affect your business as well. Softer metrics such as "the likelihood to offer a reference" or "understanding your value proposition" are tough to gauge from conversations with your client base, but oh how powerfully they impact your enterprise value. In your investor's eyes, a purchase that includes a devoted customer base is worth far more than one with only capital assets.

Market Quiz

(Circle one answer per question.)

Customers

1. Of all of your customers/clients, you know your total revenues generated this past year on:

Fewer than 5 of them   Your top 5–25   More than the top 25

2. Of this same select group, do you know what % each contributes to your total revenue?

Not sure   Approximately   Exactly

3. And you know your *real* gross profit dollars of:

Fewer than 5 of them   The top 5–25   More than the top 25

4. Of your top 25 accounts, do you know how many different times you sold them a new product/service this past year?

Not sure   Approximately   Exactly

5. In general, do you know why your customers buy from your company versus your competition?

No   Not sure   Yes

Product/Services

1. The unique selling proposition of your company is:

Unknown to your customers   Known by your customers

The reason they are customers

2. Of your top products/services/billable hours, you know the total revenue generated this past year of:

Fewer than 5 of them   The top 5–25   More than the top 25

3. Of these same items, do you know what % of your revenues each creates?

        Not sure   Approximately   Exactly

4. Of your top products/services/billable hours, do you know how many of each were sold this past year?

        Not sure   Approximately   Exactly

5. Of these same items, you know the *real* gross profit dollars and gross profit % of:

Fewer than 5 of them   The top 5–25   More than the top 25

For the ten questions above, give yourself a score value of -1 for every answer you circled in the first column, any answer in the middle column give yourself a 0, and for an answer in the far right column give yourself a score value of 1. Scores of 7 or more mean that you are on the right track; below that, you have some work to do.

Your employee base is the last but perhaps one of the most important metrics, worth considerable attention on your part. The Ring$ of Value tell us that an entity with a strong cultural environment is worth more money to an investor than one with only one devoted employee—the owner. This powerful cultural model begins when your employees feel a sense of ownership in what they are contributing to the organization. When they know you care about them, and when they know they are valued, they will go that extra mile, which will translate to your P with simultaneously increases to V, which means suitors will then take notice.

Employee Quiz

(Circle one answer per question.)

1. As a dollar amount, what direction is your revenue per employee going?

Not sure   Decreasing   Increasing

2. For the key positions in your company, do you have sufficient bench strength for a successful continuation strategy?

Not sure   No   Yes

3. What is the date of your most recent employee handbook?

We don't have one   Not sure   Within the last 3 years

4. For how many of your employees can you name their hobby or spouse's/child's name?

None   A few   Most

5. What % of revenues do you allocate to employee education/training?

None   Don't know   Over 1%

For the five questions above, give yourself a score value of -1 for every answer you circled in the first column, any answer in the middle column give yourself a 0, and for an answer in the far right column give yourself a score value of 1. Scores of 4 or more mean that you are on the right track (the scores for this quiz should be high); below that, you have some work to do.

Now add up all of your scores from all seven sections (a total of 35 questions) and find your overall knowledge result within the ranges below:

25–35 Congratulations, you know your company very well and are ready for the Rings!

15–24 You are performing at about industry average; tune up in some areas before you fully engage in the Rings.

< 15 You have lots of P and V waiting to be realized once you improve your metric knowledge!

At the core, your depth of understanding of your competition, your industry's best practices, your employees, but mostly your understanding of yourself will determine your ability to pivot away from danger. It will enable your enterprise to grow, or your lack of understanding can cripple your potential.

I see so many business owners who choose not to be aware of their own metrics. Whether this is from lack of time, arrogance, or ignorance, I cannot say. However, my experiences with acquisitions have shown me that the reasons really don't matter. The fact is, businesses without these guiding metrics and principles are just worth less. Period!

Chapter 7 Takeaways

1. Most business owners fail to use the data already available to them in a meaningful way; how well did you score on this self-evaluation quiz?

2. The more finely tuned your financial literacy and goal tracking, the more comfortable it will be for you to allow your trusted employees to handle the day-to-day business noise, thus finally freeing you up to visualize real value opportunities in the Ring$ of Value to really boost overall value.

3. Develop three metrics from each of the seven quiz sections in this chapter. Track and use the results to impact change on your performance ratios, and then watch how those changes can drive your company's future valuation!

CHAPTER 8

GET YOUR STOCK MOVING

"I used to think of [Steve Jobs] as this romantic, a lone inventor,
until I realized that his most perfect creations were the result of
being surrounded by an extraordinary team." —Walter Isaacson, *The
Innovators*

A s you have been reading this book, you've probably been
thinking, "How in the world am I supposed to fit in all this
extra work?" I get it. Concentrating on the Rings while being cog-
nizant of and owning your responsibilities within the daily business noise is more than one person can do without help. No one
is suggesting all of this work is yours alone, in fact just the opposite. Just as Steve Jobs invited brilliant talent inside his circle
and allowed those contributors to run with their ideas, your company is far more valuable when it includes a team of collabora-
tors. Appropriate delegation and teamwork can help you maximize your corporate earnings while simultaneously adding value
to your company through the Rings.

Beyond that, the old top-down hierarchy is a stale model in
today's business climate because it just doesn't take into consideration how younger generations prefer to work. While wages are
absolutely still a factor to the younger workforce, the opportunity
to make a difference in a company and its impact on the world

rank among Millennials' top priorities in workplace surveys. Be aware, dated dictatorial models are a red flag to modern investors because buyers like to see depth in key positions and some youth sprinkled throughout management.

Ironically, by backing off some on the "we do things my way around here" lever, your company may actually grow beyond your current expectations. If you create a space where employees feel valued and invested in you and the company, then you begin to draw a higher caliber of talent, your reputation in the marketplace is enhanced, and that employee base progression will prosper. A sophisticated management structure is a sign of a thriving, desirable enterprise, and according to Ring #7: Cultural Environment, it can actually enhance the overall value of the organization.

The moment you realize that you don't have to do every single task yourself may just be the day that you yourself become more valuable to the business and your business becomes more valuable too. Conversely, your company's growth is very likely being constrained by the idea that you are the only one who can complete key work functions. Allowing your employees to take ownership of their segments shows your potential buyer that you have built a solid, respected team that will perpetuate with or without you. As a result of your trust, these key players *want to work for you and your company*. Best of all, you are now free to work on the company's Rings. Allowing yourself this kind of freedom is a win-win situation for sure.

It takes a significant investment of time to hire and train the right employees who then own key functions of your business. So holding on to those people is crucial, because, as you now know, the cost to replace them can be as much as five to fifteen times their annual salary. To help motivate and retain those key employees, I encourage you to take a look at creative company stock ownership solutions.

Your Stock as a Motivator

Some companies "get their stock moving" by offering it as incentive to key employees. By stock, we're referring to actual ownership of common stock shares in the company. Stock ownership transfers aren't just for large corporations. Small and medium-sized businesses can use them effectively too. **Stock doesn't have to be traded on a market or even require an outside valuation to be bought, sold, or transferred within a company.**

This use of stock has two advantages. First, it helps capture employee loyalty and increases the likelihood they'll be with the company long enough to realize the stock-value appreciation and thus, the increase in their own personal worth. Second, and lesser known, it demonstrates to your future investors that your company's stock is active and valuable. This equity value has been reinforced *because* someone other than you has bought it or received value from it in the form of compensation. Either way, it can be encouraging to an outside investor to the see the company stock in more than just one person's hands.

Additionally, the efforts of the top employees you've chosen to share in the ownership have a direct effect on several of your Rings, so you are not trying to do it all yourself. We've already mentioned building a desirable cultural environment, Ring #7, as one very important valuation achievement. Well, let's say your key employee is a supply chain genius (Ring #4, Distribution Channels). By allowing him or her some ownership in the company, your opportunity for profit and value expands—probably by much more than the percentage of stock you shared.

Or, let's look at another example. Going back to our fictitious veterinarian practice, let's say you hire a specialist vet to cater specifically to the boom of backyard chicken owners. All of a sudden, your practice has expanded its client base by 20 percent. Ring #3, Branding and Public Identification, starts expanding because no one else in the community can serve these particular pet owners, and you haven't really had to do any extra work. So this new vet has enhanced your profitability, enhanced the culture, and enhanced the marketing power of your enterprise. Plus, this addition frees you up conceptually to work on your own core competency. Wouldn't it be smart to vest that new teammate in your business at the cost of giving up some of your ownership? Isn't owning 100 percent of a tiny venture less valuable than owning something more valuable in the aggregate?

From My Experience
Embracing Creative Thought

When I made the switch from being a CPA in the public accounting field to serving as CFO at Willitts Designs, the gift and collectibles company, the culture difference was night and day. Being a CPA is buttoned-down seriousness. Willitts Designs embraced free thinking and creativity. While both styles can be effectively utilized, the Willitts' model was far more appealing to my own entrepreneurial side.

The company CEO, Bill Willitts, encouraged creativity and rewarded key players with stock, though he always maintained a more than 50 percent ownership position for expediency in the corporate decision-making process and for documentation purposes.

When I first arrived there, Bill owned 55 percent and his three other partners owned 15 percent each. As key business partners, they each headed a broad department within the company: sales, product sourcing and licensing, and operations. He didn't *have* to share the ownership, but Bill was well before his time. His very simple yet powerful business philosophy was "It is far more productive and easier getting things done with others helping to pull on the same rope as you are." Not to mention, it's a lot more constructive, creative, fun, and a whole lot less lonely at the top of a company that employs this philosophy. (You sole business owners know what I am referring to here.)

I recognize that for some entrepreneurs, the idea of sharing the ownership of their carefully tended company seems like giving something up rather than gaining something. If you think that way, you are not alone, but that doesn't make the supposition correct. It is commonly understood that a strong and deep employee base can increase profitability through a stable, trained workforce and less turnover. Beyond that, this positive cultural environment (Ring #7) can increase the M of an organization versus its industry competitors, which then increases the V! It's a win-win-win scenario for you, your employees, and your company's value. If you have employees (or potential employees) whom you know could help you increase your company's V, then for the sake of your own equity value, shouldn't you be looking at ways to "**get your company stock moving**"?

If that is not enough incentive, think of it from a prospective buyer's point of view. If you can show that the ownership of the business goes beyond you and/or your family and is diverse and deep, all of that is a value enhancement. It is an intangible, but it is good for a buyer to know that your stock is worth something to others too.

So, since that old constrictive approach of holding on tight to those shares of stock is probably equally as constrictive on the growth and value of the corporate stock, let's look at some employee motivation and retention mechanisms available to you now by using just some of the built-up equity in your company's current stock. To be a true value enhancer, it is important to view awarding equity as part of a continuing program that will be available to future employees, not simply as a single transaction.

While this is not tax advice, the following is a brief overview of five such popular stock ownership transfer methods. I strongly recommend working with a financial professional to ensure your equity transfer is set up correctly so that you achieve the most value for any stock moves that you make.

Gifting – Yes, you can simply give your corporate stock away. While typically done with family members, this approach is available for broader use as well and can be a great tool to provide stock quickly and economically to the recipient. Obviously, as the one making the gift, you don't receive any direct compensation back. However, if done tactically, this equity transfer can be an effective tool to help you build your leadership team for years to come.

Personal Purchase – This is the typical scenario, where an individual buyer simply purchases shares of stock. Here, the company or an existing owner sells part of its/his/her stock ownership to someone else, who then will own those shares. These transactions can occur with a single payment or a series of payments, which may help the cash flow of the buyer and the timing of the income recognition for the seller.

Stock Bonus – Generally part of an incentive plan to help reward performance and drive value, companies can offer bonuses to recipients in their own corporate stock (versus cash). Stock bonuses can give valuable employees a way to get their foot in the door to ownership while tying them closer to the company. These stock bonuses are awarded and taxed like any cash bonus, except they are not liquid like a typical payroll-type bonus would be. The clever component of a stock bonus from the company's perspective is that while it is treated as a deductible expense on the books, no actual cash outlay is made. So it becomes a *non-cash* corporate deduction!

Stock Options – This vehicle allows select recipients an opportunity to purchase stock at a fixed price during a fixed period of time. This form of stock ownership motivates employees to drive the company's growth in revenue and value, since over time they have the ability to participate in its improved performance. Here's how stock options work. Say an option is granted (no money is transferred yet) to an employee to purchase a portion of company's stock at its current value. This individual then has the option to purchase that stock any time over the stated period of time, say ten years. If the value of the stock goes up, the employee can then exercise the option by acquiring the stock back at its early established value yet selling it at the now higher price!

Employee Stock Ownership Plan (ESOP) – Here, an owner sells or the company issues new shares to the ESOP trust, which is an entity effectively made up of all of the company's employees. Over time, these shares are then allocated to these qualified employees through the ESOP entity. The theory is that an ESOP will generally allow ownership among all of the company employees, thus providing a broader benefit and motivator than the more individually isolated alternatives outlined above. Talk about having a lot of motivated employee hands pulling on that same rope!

My experience with implementing ESOP plans is that a lot of owners have fear of the unknown, which tends to stop them from pursuing this viable option. All they hear is that ESOPs are highly regulated, very complex, and involve significant planning and costs. All of which is true. However, think of those considerations just as barriers to entry. Once you make it through, ESOPs can be a fantastic employee motivator, allow the owner to take some equity off the table, and provide a vehicle to really get the stock moving! Oh, and once installed, both the *principal and interest payments* on the stock transaction debt are fully deductible by the company—what a powerful tax benefit!

As a recipient of most of these types of stock transfers throughout my career, I can tell you that these are very effective motivators for employees, as they enhance performance and encourage participation in additional future ownership opportunities—all the while adding value to the enterprise. Envision how much power comes from your whole team pulling hard together to reach a mutually beneficial goal. It's exciting to see happen, and fun to be a part of.

In business, you can't do it all alone, nor do you really want to. By transferring some amount of your company's stock—even just a few percentage points—to an employee who gets results, it has been my experience that you will actually increase your corporate value faster than if you don't move your stock.

You see, getting your stock moving is really self-serving. Your employee recipients have to earn that privilege with their hard work. The value they bring with that hard work increases the worth of company stock—a boon to all the stockholders, including you.

One final thought, and perhaps the most important: Incentives like these are a tool you can use to gain back some of your precious time . . . time you can use to build even more value in the Rings.

Work *on* Not *in* Your Business

All through our discussions of the Rings, you may have been saying to yourself, "Sounds good, but I've only got two hands and 24 hours in a day." One word will save your sanity and quality of life: delegation. I have said you can't delegate the knowledge of what happens in crucial aspects of your company such as the financial statements, but remember that you can ask others to prepare them. You can, as in the example above, give responsibility for execution of an entire Ring to a trusted employee or partner. Let your branding expert handle the marketing while you reserve one day a week to push forward in your own area of expertise. Here is a thought: Once you are able to shift some of your current duties, reserve your Fridays or the first few hours of every day for Ring$ of Value efforts. Just 20 percent of your time can go toward building the qualities that will exponentially expand your value. Isn't that much time worth the potential benefits? I know it will be—**just try it!**

Going hand in hand with delegation is trust. You have to trust that someone else can perform as well as you would. Perhaps differently, but perform really well nonetheless. Here's how you avoid the ulcers some get from delegation. Combine the ingredients of trust and delegation with a chaser of verification. Trust that you have made the right decision in putting someone else in your place to run the department or project, but verify it too! Just like with financial knowledge, as CEO you can trust but you do not get to delegate the ultimate responsibility. So in summary: **Trust, delegate, but verify.**

To add one final piece to this theme, what if there is a Ring opportunity but you the owner just don't have that particular skill set or time to grab it? Perhaps it is a new product or service that would dovetail into an existing business model or be the basis for a whole new concept. You feel it could be a big hit and perhaps even result in a new revenue stream (Ring #5), but you have no idea where to start. Then what? Is it a dead Ring? Nope, no such thing. You tap this resource within your existing employee base or hire an expert and offer him or her incentive with some stock options, and watch what happens. With your direction and leadership along with your key employee's know-how, the Ring becomes reality and the company value takes flight.

When you can put down the to-do list and concentrate on being the visionary of your company, this newfound freedom can not only be reinvigorating but valuable! That's the power of sharing the burden, and that's why you want to include trusted employees inside your circle of ownership.

Chapter 8 Takeaways

1. Stock options, transfers, and programs aren't just for large corporations. Small and medium-sized businesses can realize financial benefits from using these value-enhancing tools too.

2. There are a number of ways to use stock to motivate and retain key employees—try one or two of them.

3. Get your stock moving and watch your company's value increase!

CHAPTER 9

THINK LIKE A BUYER

Yes, you read that correctly: Think like a buyer, not a seller, to increase your company's value. Putting yourself in your buyer's shoes not only may allow you to run your business more efficiently, there are also larger benefits that many selling owners miss out on due to a failure to anticipate changes that their buyer may be going to make. Worst of all, those changes translate to extra profits for the buyer from a higher valuation down the road, when they are ready to resell the entity. All because the seller had tunnel vision and continued to look at the business the way it was versus taking the view that an excited buyer sees, which is one of endless opportunities.

Defining Terms and Conditions

Before we analyze further the distinctly different mindsets between sellers and buyers, we need to explain the difference between enterprise value and equity value. I know, I know. You're already yawning. Hold on. I will be brief, but this is another technical area that you need to really understand so that you don't leave money on the table. Enterprise value is the total value of your business, or the V in our valuation formula, which includes debt. (To simplify this discussion, we will not consider the impact of cash on this definition.) Whereas equity value is our formula V minus debt. Or simply, Enterprise Value - Equity Value = Debt.

Numerically, then, no matter how a company is financed, its enterprise value stays the same. Equity value, however, will change depending on the change in debt structure. The key take-away point here is to know the terminology so you understand whether the buyer is referring to your enterprise value or equity value.

To better visualize how big a difference it could be, let's look at this definition through a simpler example, again like selling a house. If you sell a house for $1,000,000 that has a $600,000 mortgage attached to it, the enterprise value is the $1,000,000 sales price, yet the equity value is $400,000 (the $1,000,000 selling price less the $600,000 mortgage). In a business context, simply insert a company value in the above example and the mortgage would be the related debt.

As you can see, depending on your debt position, this could potentially be a very big difference!

Why is understanding the distinction in terms so important? Well, there are at least a couple of critical reasons to understand the definitional differences between the two valuation directions:

• When comparing multiples and valuation prices in your own industry, it is very important to know which terminology (enterprise or equity) your peers and competitors are using when you are comparing this information to yours.

• **It is financially critical that you and your prospective buyer are talking the same language** ("apples to apples") in your valuation approaches. You don't want to be calculating your bottom line thinking they are taking on the debt of your company if they are thinking the opposite!

One final note: Since each company will have its own debt structure on its balance sheet and since the enterprise value approach does not make any adjustments for debt, this method is considered a more objective standard when comparing companies across a sector.

Internal versus External Transactions

Like valuation models themselves, people's impetuses for selling their companies also vary. Let's break them down into either a valuation for an internal sale or one for an external transaction. There's a world of difference between the two, but the biggest influencer on the two types is the question, **what is the purpose of this transaction?** The answer to this very important question will also directly impact the valuation.

An internal valuation approach represents a philosophy that is often designed for sales between existing owners and/or employees, related party transactions, transfers of ownership from parents to their children, or a perpetuation plan of some sort. This approach is generally used within some type of succession plan where the objective is not to wring every last cent out of a transaction. Rather, the internal transition of ownership is more valuable than receiving the highest possible price for the business from an outsider. An example of an internal valuation is the formula you might use for your buy/sell agreement within your company if you have more than one owner in your company. Quite often in these cases, the pricing multiple is set at a discounted rate or capped between the owners for an internal transfer versus what would be available in the open market. **(A side note: If your company has multiple owners, please make sure you have an up-to-date buy/sell agreement.)**

The opposite of an internal valuation formula is an external valuation, which is utilized in third-party transactions or those performed at arm's length. These valuations are not for the purposes of internal succession, rather they are for outright sales and thus they have no implied formula-driven price ceiling.

In your daily business, I am sure you feel you run your company fairly efficiently. Meaning, as part of your normal senior management process you now regularly review your current financial results and metrics versus plan, prior year, and your industry comparables. You use these to make the continuous changes necessary to adjust along the way. However, deep down you know that there are additional changes that you would and could make if you had the time and resources to act on them. This is a pretty typical situation, by the way; there is never enough time in a day to get everything done. But what changes would a buyer make with enough time and money? Moreover, what impact would those changes have on the company's value?

Let's take a look at the numerical impact between an internal and external pro forma calculation. As you will see, the differences are stark!

To start this visual comparison, let's recall our Mountaintop Ski & Sports retail store from Chapter 6 and our valuation formula $V = P \times M + E$.

Using key financial information from those earlier financial reports, the company's stated P, or EBITDA, from its income statement was $200,000 and the total equity from its balance sheet shows $400,000. Let's also assume the M is two. Therefore, as presented, the V would equal:

MOUNTAINTOP SKI & SPORTS
Initial Business Valuation

EBITDA	$200,000
Multiple	x 2
Value of Operations	400,000
Equity/TNW	400,000
Total Business Value	$800,000

Pretty good amount for that business, right?

Do you think the owners would sell the business for $800,000? Well, let's continue this example and you answer that question for yourself.

Let's now assume in this second example that Mountaintop Ski & Sports is owned by two 50/50 owners. One of the two owners is requesting a buyout by the other owner under their previously agreed upon buy/sell formula. Further, let's assume the terms of the buy/sell formula call for a valuation based on a pro forma income statement. (To pro forma your income statements means to normalize them for expected changes that you know of, or for changes that you expect to make. Then, you project them forward, assuming all events will be realized.) So in our example, the departing owner's payroll (let's assume $200,000) will no longer be included in the business operating costs, yet an allotment for a lesser-paid employee (say $100,000) is factored in its place. As we now know, if numerical change is realizable, then this lower net wage difference can be projected going forward in a pro forma income statement. By assuming those changes, the following internal business valuation calculation would show an overall increase in EBITDA and a new valuation based on a pro forma net $100,000 reduction in payroll costs (assuming a $200,000 owner salary less $100,000 for the replacement):

MOUNTAINTOP SKI & SPORTS
Internal Business Valuation

	Initial Valuation	Pro forma Adjustments	Internal Valuation
EBITDA	$200,000	$100,000	$300,000
Multiple	x 2	x 2	x 2
Value of Operations	400,000	200,000	600,000
Equity/TNW	400,000	N/C	400,000
Total Business Value	$800,000	$200,000	$1,000,000

As we now know from earlier discussions, any change in EBITDA will then be extended by the company's multiplier to reflect an overall change in valuation.

So, based on this $100,000 net reduction in payroll, EBITDA went up $100,000 and the newly adjusted P is now multiplied by the same M of two. As a result, the initial valuation of $800,000 went up $200,000 to a new internally adjusted valuation of $1,000,000.

That is an example of the impact for any pro forma change in P. That is, the new pro forma P is then multiplied by your respective M. As you can see by the drastic change in value, this is very, very powerful valuation knowledge for you to have!

However, even given those initial and pro forma internal mathematics, an experienced buyer would still be perfectly content paying that $1,000,000 purchase price.

Why? Because a financial buyer is thinking of the selling (or their exit) opportunities as they are considering the purchase! It's a whole different way of looking at a transaction. **To most people, the purchase is the end of the process. To financial buyers, the purchase is the beginning.** In their world, a purchase leads to a sale, then another purchase and sale, and the cycle continues. Welcome to the way they think!

Therefore, when they look to market a business for resale, they will not be bound by any buy/sell agreement formula or succession plan philosophies. In these instances, an external valuation pro forma model is developed rather than using either of those previous models.

Here's how the pros do it.

Professional Valuation Tips

An external valuation may start with your same given EBITDA amount, but by the time an experienced seller has finished their much, much, much, more aggressive pro forma EBITDA projection, the only thing that may look the same is the name of the company.

Beyond any earlier adjustments, a pro will project changes that include any new revenue activities that were not already considered in your income statements (like a new product line or an additional retail location). Further, they might exclude any salary in their pro forma for the remaining owner (assuming he or she will be bought out in the transaction). They may or may not factor in a less-costly employee. Finally, they may assume a reduction in overhead costs from better expense management.

For our example purposes, let's conservatively assume that all of the above additional "pro" forma adjustments result in an additional increase in EBITDA of $200,000. Let's further assume that with the new product lines and lower expense run rate Mountaintop Ski & Sports has so improved its projected standing in its niche that its new M is a four versus the current industry standard of two.

Now look what happens to the valuation:

MOUNTAINTOP SKI & SPORTS
External Business Valuation

	Initial Valuation	Pro forma Adjustments	Internal Valuation	"Pro" forma Adjustments	External Valuation
EBITDA	$200,000	$100,000	$300,000	$200,000	$500,000
Multiple	x 2	x 2	x 2	x 4	x 4
Value of Operations	400,000	200,000	600,000	800,000	2,000,000
Equity/TNW	400,000	N/C	400,000	N/C	400,000
Total Business Value	$800,000	$200,000	$1,000,000	$800,000	$2,400,000

From an $800,000 initial valuation to a $1,000,000 internal valuation to now a whopping $2,400,000 external valuation. That's three times the initial valuation!

As stated earlier, this futuristic picture will often be much, much different from the current reality of the business. But look at what is possible!

To better understand the impact of these pro forma mathematics, let's take a step back to really understand what the drivers are for this huge increase in value.

The secret power behind the mathematics of the multiplier is that as you improve your M, you are not just improving it on the incremental changes. Rather, you are improving the overall value realized **all the way back to dollar one**. Therefore, the much improved industry position that now earned the company a four-times multiplier is not just applied to the $200,000 of further incremental "pro" improvements. Rather, the improvement carries all the way back to the first dollar changes of the initial valuation, encompassing the entire newly projected EBITDA of $500,000 to a revised pro forma operational value of $2,000,000 and a new overall valuation of $2,400,000!

The assumption supporting this back-to-dollar-one rationale is that going forward, this entity is not that same old industry-standard, EBITDA-performing company anymore, but rather a fully revitalized EBITDA enterprise with new products, improved margins, and lower operating expense run rates.

The crazy thing is that it's not tricky math or an optical illusion; this can really happen . . . and does! The value is right there, waiting for the entrepreneurs who really understand the power of the M multiple in business valuations. Bottom line, a top-performing company is just way more valuable and saleable (just like that nicer house in the neighborhood) than one in the middle of the pack. The speed of such a transaction and the higher resulting sale prices reflect it.

Shocking but true, the Mountaintop Ski & Sports business was actually that valuable all along. Now whether or not the current owners could visualize these changes or visualize them enough to pro forma them out for their prospective buyer is something else. **More important than this example, can you see the possibility in your company?**

Well, as a soon-to-be savvy Ring$ of Value graduate, you have an opportunity to not only visualize these results but to realize those same profit potentials. You can be the one to wrap those same "pro" forma concepts into your own company's valuation and sell at a much higher price than perhaps you ever might have even thought possible. You are now armed with a new depth of understanding of your financials and the trigger points that drive a valuation. So when the right opportunity presents itself, you won't get eaten alive by a savvier buyer.

Applying what you know now about business valuation, picture an ill-prepared owner/seller promoting an internal valuation that he or she cannot support with financial data. Combine that with very skilled buyers who know full well that they will be buying the company at a discount while ultimately selling it at a market/external valuation. It kind of makes you shake your head at how much money a seller can leave on the table for a buyer, doesn't it?

Making the Tough Changes

There is a point in every sale that I refer to as "the moment the buyer shows up." This is when the new owner finally becomes fully engaged. It might be immediate, or it may take a bit of time after the honeymoon period of new ownership wears off, but trust me, it always happens. At some point, beyond changing the company colors, slogans, and operating hours, an experienced buyer will always make those tough business decisions that you either did not see or were unable to make. He or she won't agonize over it like you might have, and yet will reap the rewards that you didn't. That is because at some point **the buyer always shows up** and wants a return on investment.

Regardless of whether the seller prepared a pro forma income statement as a selling tool or not, the experienced buyer will. And, because the buyer is tracking ROI, his or her pro forma version will be far more aggressive than you ever imagined yours to be. A buyer's projections, then, at least in the short run, become the operational roadmap for the company under this new ownership. Under this new owner, these pro forma assumptions have a very high likelihood of becoming reality.

You may think the idea of finding new revenue streams, new products or services, or overall expense efficiencies is not achievable. Impossible for a company that size, you might even say. You can't hit a target you don't have; imagine what a new buyer might do with this opportunity. What would their Rings of Value be?

Remember, "Think Like a Buyer"

Now do the pro forma valuation exercise. What changes would you make if you were your own buyer?

With you as the hypothetical new owner in charge, those new products or services that never got off the drawing board now have ownership backing—backing that was not there when you ran things before. And what a surprise, those new ideas are now making a significant impact on total revenues.

Processes and technology are being upgraded to be able to handle the increased volume more effectively, and at less-incremental costs.

Suddenly those extra overhead positions that were justified for years are all gone. This includes that extra layer of management and the soon-to-retire staff. Expect the new owners to eliminate all redundant positions and consolidate extraneous locations. Ditto for extra administrative services.

In other words, when seasoned buyers shows up—and they will—they won't run the business with the same people and processes that brought the company to the industry's mid-level standard. Instead, they'll make the changes necessary to run the business as it could have performed for you—on that pro forma basis. The ROI on new processes, technology, and products are quickly measured and implemented while those tough personnel decisions are expeditiously made. All of these end up catapulting this previously middle-of-the-road company into an industry leader worth more than two, three, or four times its earlier value.

Of course, there is an art to making some of these changes, but **mostly the art is just the act of doing!**

Now that you know these strategies, doesn't it make sense for you to be the person who benefits from those changes, painful though they may be? **Why let your buyer have your profits and valuation?**

Don't Be Average

In my career, I have noticed that companies seem to get to plateaus and get a bit static. Interestingly, this stagnant point often occurs at round revenue numbers such as $1 million, $10 million, $25 million, $50 million, $100 million, and so on. The business rises to a certain level and then stays there . . . too long. My theory for why? The same people who helped get it to that level never leave. And, as the saying goes, **What got you here won't get you there.** In other words, different people bring different skill sets to an organization. To reach that next level, a company requires sharper processes, more strategic thinking—which often means just better people, **ones who can make your company go faster**.

This is why Ring of Value #7 is so important. Build a cultural environment where new ideas and critical thinking are encouraged. Offering your products or services the same old way, using outdated processes time and again, "because it's the way we've always done it," is why profits can stagnate or worse yet retreat. Hanging onto staff members who no longer contribute to their pay value because they've always been there is certainly understandable from a loyalty perspective. However, sometimes it is those very people who slow the business today, making it harder for your business to change and thrive into the future.

Though it's hard to acknowledge, sometimes the biggest culprit is the business owner. Paradoxically, the very people who created the entity can be the same people who impede its further success.

Michael Dell, founder of Dell computers, said in a 2003 graduation speech at the University of Texas: "Try never to be the smartest person in the room. And if you are, I suggest you invite smarter people . . . or find a different room." Although Dell was speaking to new graduates, I think this quote applies even more to business owners, because we really don't want to be the people with all the answers. First, it's a lot of responsibility to shoulder on your own. More important, it vastly limits innovation. That top-down model is really just one brain tackling thousands of problems. By assembling a team of diverse, creative thinkers and allowing them to speak and take ownership of new ventures, your company can only be the better for it.

A final thought. Right now you might be asking yourself, why do I have to be the one to go through and make all the difficult changes?—changes that you already know deep down you should have made by now. Wouldn't it be smart to just pro forma them into my valuation? Won't the buyer then pay me as if I did make them? Nice try, but the reality is that actual results carry far more weight in valuations than pro forma projections. Beyond that, once your business actually achieves this new level of performance, suddenly further opportunities open up and become evident. Now that next pro forma valuation is even higher!

Bottom line, it's better for you to just make those changes today and realize your own additional valuation profits!

Chapter 9 Takeaways

1. As efficiently as you may run your company today, remember that a buyer will be looking for innovation and forward-thinking that separates the company not just from the competition but from companies in a breadth of industries. The Ring$ of Value provide that "think like a buyer" progressive thought process.

2. Improving value is for the owners and entrepreneurs who really understand the power of the M multiple in business valuations. Practice to become proficient in calculating your company's EBITDA, pro forma income statement, and business valuation.

3. Don't be average. Don't settle for the status quo, even if the status quo is providing you with a good living. Stay excited and engaged in the business you have built. Make the tough decisions so that you financially benefit from them—not your buyer. Set your sights on the target—set your sights on the Ring$ of Value.

CHAPTER 10

PULLING IT ALL TOGETHER

My purpose in writing *Ring$ of Value: Run Your Business Every Day Like It's For Sale* started with a lightbulb moment. Throughout my experience in business transactions, I have heard about owners of businesses of all sizes losing money on deal after deal. In the mergers and acquisitions world, I also heard that those who didn't hire a pricey advisor left money on the table because they didn't understand the valuation formula or the drivers to that business valuation. The thing is, the simplified formula presented in this book can be used by any CEO, division head, or manager to run a valuation calculation similar to what an expert would do, and do it within minutes or perhaps even seconds, if they only knew how. That's where this book started, with the desire to share that insider knowledge—to let you in on those well-kept business valuation secrets.

As the book started taking shape, I realized that the most successful companies have very specific attributes in common. If incorporated, those attributes could ignite any business's valuation because those entities would have their own unique multiplier—one that would be higher than their competitors'. These common attributes are how the Ring$ of Value came into being. By carving out time to understand the valuation process and drivers, *you too* can realize the same types of successful transactions that I have been associated with. So that's the gist of this book: **Understand the valuation formula plus know the valuation drivers—the Ring$ of Value.**

I also wrote this book from the vantage point of a very experienced business professional. We all know that some companies fail. What I also know is that they are not all failing from bad ideas or an underdeveloped market but from *a lack of financial savvy*. The business lessons included in this book are so crucial because they go hand in hand with your understanding of the valuation formula and ultimately the exponential impact each Ring can have on your enterprise. These lessons are included to guide you around the pitfalls that others have succumbed to.

In this final chapter, I also want to spend a bit more time explaining why I subtitled this text *Run Your Business Every Day Like It's For Sale.* What do I mean by that? Why would I want you to operate your company like you are trying to sell it? It's not that I want you to have an eye on the door. Rather, I think that mindset will enable you to run your company better.

It is understandable to get stuck in routines or mentally lose your business focus at times. Coming and going to work the same way, not *really* concentrating on every key decision being made, delegating duties that perhaps shouldn't be delegated, spending too much time following industry trends versus trying to lead them—the list goes on and on. I understand; it happens. At moments like this, ask yourself, Would you be doing things differently if you were considering selling the business? Would you have made that choice rather than another if there was a transaction looming? What would that potential buyer/investor think of the decision? How much value was added by this move or that one? Keeping the image of a potential buyer or investor in the back of your mind will immediately add energy and direction to your business compass, all the while making you and your company better for it. Using our visual Ring$ of Value target as your guide will undoubtedly help you craft big decisions that will add value to your company.

Even the thought of a potential transaction can help focus efforts. To illustrate, let's think about our house-selling example again. You have probably already experienced selling residential property and all the work that precedes a transaction. The inspections indicate areas of concern or build trust for the potential investor. If problems are revealed, they are going to be an issue or price concession in the due diligence process. Proactive repairs, fresh carpet, and new paint all serve as a parallel to having every aspect of your business performing at its optimal performance level. If all of your team, departments, and processes are organized and flow seamlessly together, that is attractive to your buyer. And just like with selling a house, keeping these key assets in tip-top shape all the time adds value to the sale price, because small problems never have a chance to become big financial deductions in your negotiations.

If you have actively run your business every day like it's for sale, you'll have ready answers to questions about your internal metrics and ratios too. A buyer will assume that you, the owner, are fully fluent in all your own performance measures. And, as a graduate of the Ring$ of Value business valuation program, you do! If not, consider yourself warned, because those *Shark Tank–* type questions are coming.

Your buyer will also expect to see your corporate documents up to date and *immediately* available for their due diligence process. Having your legal house in order is a soothing point for a buyer, who at that point in the process will definitely not want to have any undisclosed or out-of-date corporate document issues surface. As I said earlier, when United GreenMark sold to John Deere, two things permitted the company to de-emphasize steps in its due diligence process: how complete and up-to-date the corporate and financial documentation were, and the immediate availability of those documents. These elements increased John

Deere's trust in the transaction and in us. In that instance, trust really was money.

Documents and Qualities Your Company Should Have

1. Does your company have a mission statement? Mission statements plainly explain what the company's direction is right now and how it is different from the rest. These statements define the purpose and primary objectives related to your customer needs and team values. It answers the questions "What do we do?" and "What makes us different?" If you already have a mission statement, good for you, but is it current? Your statement may need to evolve alongside your evolving business, but it still should tie back to your core values. Finally, do you, your customers, and employees know and believe it? To put this emphasis into words, are you actually doing what you say you do?

2. Do you have a vision statement for the business? Vision statements are different from mission statements, as vision statements define where you want to be in the future instead of where you are currently. This statement communicates both the purpose and values of the business. It answers the question "Where do we want to be?" This statement aligns with Ring #1, Power to Change Lives in that your vision combines your core values with the broader good you are fulfilling.

3. Who on the team is charged with activating your company's mission and vision? As we have said before, you want A-level people (Ring #7, Cultural Environmen) who rise to the challenges you set, who bring fresh energy and ideas. You want people who enjoy coming to work and tell to their friends so; A-level employees have A-level friends. Further, from a buyer's or investor's perspective, the documentation in their personnel files needs to be complete and clean for inspections. While no one likes shuffling paper, having periodic evaluations, documentation of raises, commendations, and disciplinary actions neatly located in one

place, or better yet on one high-tech software platform, makes the business of employee performance easier for you to manage and accessible to anyone who will need to view these records.

4. Do you have a succession plan? Hopefully major changes in your company's leadership will be the result of careful planning, and yet disasters and major health problems happen. Don't leave your spouse, your executive team, or employees unprepared to keep the business afloat by failing to plan. Plus, a good succession plan can provide answers about what level of income the business will need in order to sustain itself, as well as what kinds of expenses may be incurred with any significant change in leadership roles.

5. Corporate documents should include your articles of incorporation if you are a C or an S corporation. If you are an LLC, you must have articles of organization, bylaws, *and all types of corporations should have minutes of all board meetings.* When is the last time real board minutes were recorded? Who is on your board and who are your directors besides you and your spouse? Do those individuals add value? If not, then perhaps today is a good day to make a change. Like everything you are doing, board members need to add real value to the organization.

Do you have a business plan? Is it updated and current? In addition to your business goals and the detailed map for reaching those goals, does your plan include your three- to five-year financial projections? Did you know that investors look for annual returns in that same timeframe? Having documented proof that you are already paralleling those three- to five-year models will show investors that you are in their sphere of business acumen relative to your business. Impressions like that matter.

Are your corporate accounting records clean? Are they *really* clean, or do they have gray items? If I came to your office today would I find any questionable income or expense items? Even if your gray items don't ultimately become tangible valuation deductions, they will taint the impression of your buyer or potential business partner. You don't want integrity issues surfacing when a buyer is reviewing your records. So do the right thing with your financial records; clean up the gray items so someone else doesn't have to. If you see a business transaction in your future, have an outside audit or review of your books done for a few years leading up to the sale—the increase in your credibility will be money well spent.

8. Are your revenue streams and marketing strategies aligned and still relevant? This really means, do your customers still want what you are selling? How can you tell? Well, if your products or services are still connecting with your target markets, then your answer will be yes and will be validated by your sales and margins, which should remain steady or even better be rising. If not, there is some work to do. Those metrics will tell you the real story.

Word to the Wise – Be Aware

Even if your products or services and marketing are right on target, be aware because nothing is guaranteed. The market is changing so very fast now. And it's not just limited to challenges from your direct competition. The very nature of innovation is changing; now threats are not *just* from your industry but from outside your industry as well. Consider disruptive innovation, which is innovation that creates a new market or value that eventually disrupts an existing market, for example what AirBnB and Uber did to the lodging and taxi industries. Look around, be open to new ideas, most important BE AWARE! Unless you are paying close attention to the market and how your products or services are performing (both in sales and margin), the niche you thought you had carved out can evaporate in the blink of an eye. This is true for consumer products, service businesses, and certainly the fashion and the food and beverage industries. Consumer trends pivot so rapidly that no business is ever perfectly safe. When is the last time you asked your customers what they want versus what you sell them? Businesses that successfully fend off these industry disruptors will need to be spinning several Rings simultaneously.

9. How do your customers feel about you, your integrity, your company, and your products or services? When is the last time you asked them for their opinions? Overpromising in order to obtain a sale may gain a few more dollars in the moment, but that strategy usually backfires because disappointing interactions are rarely repeated. Integrity means honesty and trust. It takes years to build and moments to destroy. So ensure that you, the leader, and all of your coworkers know and follow the company's code of ethics. Your name in the community and industry is one of the most valuable assets you own.

10. Are your customers able to actually transact on your website? If you can't collect revenue via your website, count on losing sales from those customers you worked so long to get. That goes for mobile-readiness too. Today's consumers have a lot of options, a lot to keep track of, and are probably taking care of their business with you between afternoon meetings and other commitments. If patronizing your business means waiting until they can get to a PC or—heaven forbid—calling you on the phone, you can forget about that sale in the future. Although technology is moving business faster than the speed of imagination, *if* your company isn't keeping pace with the transaction options that are developing then you can kiss your future profits goodbye. There is a saying that "customers are loyal as long as you are the lowest price." You can now add the phrase "and buying from you isn't time consuming or technologically difficult!"

Having these readiness documents and qualities will make you and your business better, separate you from others in your space, build a sense of professionalism in any forthcoming transaction, and all the while prove that you actually do *Run Your Business Every Day Like It's For Sale.*

Wrap-Up

As we wrap up our journey, first of all thank you for your commitment to working through this book. Neither the topics nor the results are for the average businessperson, so **congratulations to you and your company for not being average**.

I would also like to add one more caution—one last word to the wise. The most common mistake I see in business stretches across the spectrum, and it really has nothing to do with a lack of focus or financial statements. Yet it's a crippling fault. It typically reveals itself when people tell me, "Yeah, I know that" or "We don't need to have those (insert new idea)." From small businesses to large corporations, so often the people I speak to refuse to acknowledge that they may have something new to learn. They are threatened by a new idea or suggestion of change. I'm talking about unconscious incompetence, which in psychology is one of the four stages of competence. The unconscious incompetent is the one who does not understand something and, at the same time, does not recognize his or her own deficiency. Or, they may deny the usefulness of the skill entirely.

When people feel like they have to be the smartest person in the room, they fail to recognize opportunities for personal growth. To remedy this, individuals must first recognize that knowledge is a continuum, and second, they must see the value they can add to themselves and/or their company with this new skill. Then and only then can they move on. The length of time individuals dwell in their current position depends on the strength of their own stimulus to learn, and frankly their own stubbornness.

This isn't to say that you have to jump on every passing fad. Focus does help you reach goals. However, making the shift to a more open mind is not really that hard. Simply changing an immediate no to "tell me more about that" gives you the time to hear more detail and consider the possibilities. Keeping an open mind exposes you and your business to a much broader spectrum of ideas, which can all be business valuation bonuses.

Assess

Now that you know how to run your business every day like it's for sale, it's time to take stock. A good way to assess your current progress starts with these three guiding questions:

- Where are you today?
- Where are you going?
- How are you going to get there?

No one gets ahead without setting goals; remember, you can't hit a target you don't have. So right here, right now, identify your weak areas based on what you have learned in this book. Pick one area of business noise to rid yourself of and one Ring that you can start working on immediately. Then, make a plan. Break the goals into manageable steps and get to work!

One business noise obstacle that you could overcome or reassign is:

_____

_____

Your plan on how to transfer it is:

_____

_____

One Ring of Value that you can target is:

_____

_____

Your plan for implementing this Ring is:

_____

_____

Planning and managing the process will allow you more and more time to focus on adding even more value to the organization by working on **your next Ring$ of Value**!

In parting, I would like to conclude with the words of Thomas Edison, who said, "The value of an idea lies in the using of it." It is my sincere hope that in some way, even perhaps beyond your business, that these Ring$ of Value will inspire you and motivate you to act on your ideas.

***

Explore Your Passion, Find Your Ring, Embrace The Journey.

To help retain the lessons of the Ring$, use this page as a tear-out reference sheet to serve as a reminder of where your energy will have the most impact.

Ring$ of Value

Quick Reference Sheet

7. **Cultural Environment:** Create an environment so magnetic that A-level workers want to come to your company and want to bring their friends.

6. **Innovation:** Step beyond the status quo and lead your industry with creativity; this mindset becomes your identity.

5. **Revenue Streams:** Revenue does not have to be defined in linear terms only. Diversification can add new revenue and profits by utilizing some of the same overhead structure and costs that you are already paying for with existing operations.

4. **Distribution Channels:** A well-established logistical network quickly moves products or services from your organization to the customer. Whether through enhanced vendors or sourcing, or how you ultimately provide those goods and services to your customers, the more advanced and cost-efficient your network, the more valuable it is.

3. **Branding and Public Identification:** People don't buy what you do, they buy why you do it. Are you telling the right story to the right people? Good branding does.

2. **Ability to Replicate and Scale:** Document and track your processes so that any employee can perform them and the metrics are measurable. Then leverage those processes to increase revenue with diminishing incremental costs.

1. **Power to Change Lives:** Use your company's social consciousness crossover as a way to both change the conversation around an issue *and* translate to your income statement as a goodwill add-on valuation factor.